Praise for *GO! How to Beco[...]ssion Church*

"What's more important than the Great Commission? Unfortunately, too many churches—including the one I grew up in—a lot! This is the book that I wish the leaders in my church had read while I was growing up."
—**Daniel Im**, Director of Church Multiplication at NewChurches .com and teaching pastor

"This book exists as a faithful offering to the heartbeat of the church: the local congregation. With biblical foundations for a launching pad, *Go! How to Become a Great Commission Church* outlines tools for living out a daily, Christ-centered faith at levels that will speak to Christians of all educational or leadership backgrounds. The use of case studies gives readers a chance to place themselves within the story of the body of Christ, in order to provide connections to the Great Commission already at work in their community."
—**Steve Trefz**, Director of Wesley House of Study at Sioux Falls Seminary, Affiliate Professor at Garrett-Evangelical Theological Seminary

"Grounded in the Wesleyan tradition, while also pulling from the best of the Evangelical movement, this book pushes congregations to go beyond the typical mainline approach to evangelism and discipleship. Dr. Teasdale effortlessly weaves together foundational stories of scripture with real-world circumstances faced by the local church today. This is not a step-by-step manual for growing a church but rather a guidebook for congregations to get back on track toward participating in God's mission and purpose. This book is an excellent resource for anybody in need of creative ideas, practical tactics, biblical narratives, and Spirit-filled encouragement to more faithfully live out the call to go!"
—**Jenny Shult-Huffman**, Coordinator, Institute of Congregational Development, Wisconsin Conference, The United Methodist Church

GO!

HOW TO BECOME A
GREAT COMMISSION
CHURCH

MARK R. TEASDALE

GO! How to Become a Great Commission Church

The General Board of Higher Education and Ministry leads and serves The United Methodist Church in the recruitment, preparation, nurture, education, and support of Christian leaders—lay and clergy—for the work of making disciples of Jesus Christ for the transformation of the world. Its vision is that a new generation of Christian leaders will commit boldly to Jesus Christ and be characterized by intellectual excellence, moral integrity, spiritual courage, and holiness of heart and life. The General Board of Higher Education and Ministry of The United Methodist Church serves as an advocate for the intellectual life of the church. The Board's mission embodies the Wesleyan tradition of commitment to the education of laypersons and ordained persons by providing access to higher education for all persons.

Wesley's Foundery Books is named for the abandoned foundery (foundry) that early followers of John Wesley transformed into a church, which became the cradle of London's Methodist movement.

HIGHER EDUCATION & MINISTRY
General Board of Higher Education and Ministry
THE UNITED METHODIST CHURCH

CONTENTS

Acknowledgments   v

Introduction: Great Commission or Great Congregation?   ix

1. Retreat Forward   1
   Genesis 7:1-4; Proverbs 28:12, 28

2. Follow God's Lead   17
   Exodus 4:27, 7:15; Joshua 6:22

3. Get Consecrated   35
   Leviticus 10:9; Joshua 4:5

4. Standing Firm   51
   Nehemiah 6:10-14

5. Avoiding the Exile   71
   Isaiah 2:10, 5:13; Jeremiah 20:6; Ezekiel 12:4; Nahum 3:11

6. Reconcile with Each Other and God   93
   Matthew 5:24; Acts 6:1-7; Luke 12:58; 2 Corinthians 5:20

7. It's OK to Party!   117
Deuteronomy 32:49; Ecclesiastes 9:7-10; Isaiah 55:12

8. The Secrets of Being a Missional Congregation   143
1 Peter 3:21-22

Afterword and Additional Resources   159

Index   165

ACKNOWLEDGMENTS

This book began as I listened to a fine lecture given by Dr. Julie Duncan, associate professor of Old Testament at Garrett-Evangelical Theological Seminary. The lecture was on a passage in Ecclesiastes 9 in which the reader is exhorted to "go" enjoy life, including eating, drinking, and having sex with your spouse. I chuckled at how different the church would look if this command to *go* replaced the Great Commission. We probably would find it much easier to make converts! But this joke quickly gave way to a more serious question: What if the church didn't have to choose just one of these passages to define its participation in God's mission?

So often we see missional work based only on the Great Commission. While this passage does appropriately focus the church on the primary command of Jesus to make disciples, could it be that it also causes many congregations to become uncreative in their practice of making disciples? I think it does. We know we are supposed to baptize and teach, but often we are at a loss for how we can do more.

I believe we can revitalize our missional practices by looking at other Bible passages in which God sent God's people on a mission. Rather than seeing these other passages as disconnected or superseded by the Great Commission, we can see them as a trove of possible tactics to use while making disciples. My thanks to Julie for being my muse in sparking this thought for me.

Writing this book has been an adventure in rediscovering my Wesleyan heritage as a missionally focused, disciple-making juggernaut. Strangely, I found this not through reading Methodist literature but by delving into the Evangelical literature that deals with mission, church planting, and leadership. Evangelical scholars, practitioners, and authors (often with all three titles applying to the same individuals), have become the standard-bearers for making disciples in the West today. The mainline church owes them a debt of gratitude for picking up this work with enthusiasm and generating so many quality resources on these issues.

In meeting some of the major Evangelical figures writing about this, such as Ed Stetzer and Alan Hirsch, and in reading their material, something struck me forcefully: much of what the Evangelicals are promoting looks like what John Wesley did when he piloted the Methodist Revival in England throughout the eighteenth century. Alan even explained to me that it was learning about John Wesley that inspired his idea of developing missional incarnational communities.

I want to thank Ed and Alan, and especially Rick Richardson, who introduced me to many of these authors and their work. I thank them for their generosity with their time, their thoughtful engagement with the mission of the church, and their reawakening of my enthusiasm for Wesleyan studies as a guide for how the church can be effective in making disciples today.

I also offer my thanks to the Foundation for Evangelism and A Foundation for Theological Education, both of which are champions of Wesleyan studies, and both of which have supported me throughout my studies and career. Their work helps guarantee that Methodists will continue to become solid scholars and congregational leaders who can help move the church forward in its call to make disciples.

Writing this book has also been a rediscovery of the local congregation for me. I served for twelve years in a variety of positions in the local congregation. While I hold many of those memories and experiences dear, it was helpful to have those currently engaged in and with the local congregation guide me concerning what pastors and lay leaders are facing today. I offer thanks especially to those at Discipleship Ministries of The United Methodist Church who work hard to provide the needed resources and coaching for local congregations to obey the Great Commission. Special thanks to Dr. Heather Lear, The UMC director of evangelism, who has helped me adapt my thinking about personal evangelism to congregations.

I also want to thank the doctor of ministry students from my 2016 summer evangelism course: the Reverends Curtis Brown, Alicia Julia-Stanley, Andy Oliver, Shaun Overstreet, Brenda Presha, Bradley Stagg, and Roger Vest. Many of them will find bits and pieces of their stories mixed into the story of First Church that unfolds throughout these pages. Their openness about their ministries and willingness to share their successes and struggles did a great deal to shape this book.

Dr. Steve Trefz and Ms. Ana Teasdale read earlier versions of the manuscript, which was an act of extreme graciousness on their part. Their advocacy for you, the readers of the book you now hold, helped substantially as I figured out how to weave a semi-fictional narrative together with lessons on how a congregation can engage in mission more creatively.

Ana, who helped me navigate being a pastor in a local congregation for years, and now supports me as I seek to edify the church through my scholarship, was especially helpful. Her clear-eyed and honest assessments of what congregations are facing on the grassroots level gave me even more reason to appreciate her than I already had. Thank you for your support over the years and particularly as I wrote this book.

Finally, I want to thank Dr. Kathy Armistead for the invitation to write this book and Dr. K. K. Yeo who encouraged me to follow up on that invitation.

GREAT COMMISSION OR GREAT CONGREGATION?

It had been an exhilarating few weeks. The terror and grief we felt had been exploded by a kind of terrible, awesome joy. A man had come back from the grave! Not as a zombie or ghost but as himself—alive and active and so fully real. It was mind-bending, reality-transforming. There would have been no way for us to take it in, except that he came back and lived alongside us.

He would come and go, sometimes for short visits, sometimes for longer ones. He would meet with us one-on-one or in groups. He even would join us for meals, just like the old times, except for the slowly healing wounds visible on his body. When we were together, he would comfort and reassure us. He must have known how difficult his presence with us was for us to grasp. He would show us again and again that it really was he, alive and in the flesh. He would exhort us to believe, and seeing our struggle to do so, he would promise us that the Holy Spirit was coming and would guide us to receive the truth.

On our final day with him in the flesh, he moved among us, greeting each of us by name and offering words of grace. He then turned to address us together, telling us that all authority in heaven and earth was his. Lifting his hands in blessing, he pledged that even though he was going away from us in body, he will be with us always.

* * *

This is indeed a comforting picture of what it might have been like in the forty days following the resurrection of Christ. We can easily imagine it as a time full of hope and joy, with an amazingly powerful deity gently living alongside his beloved disciples, urging them to believe in the far greater reality God wants for them.

Did you catch what was missing from this imagined account though? The Great Commission!

As pleasant as this depiction of Jesus with his followers might be, without the Great Commission it is incomplete. The fact that Jesus commissions his disciples not just once, but at least five times in the days following his resurrection (once in each of the Gospels and once in the book of Acts: Matt 28:16-20, Mark 16:9-20, Luke 24:36-53, John 20:19-31, and Acts 1:1-11), demonstrates just how important the Great Commission is.

The Great Commission was the capstone to Jesus' earthly ministry. Jesus had been born as the incarnate Son of God to inaugurate the kingdom of God. He spent most of his ministry teaching people about the kingdom, calling them to repent and to live as his disciples. After proving the power of God to overcome evil through his suffering, death, and resurrection, Jesus handed his ministry of making disciples to his followers. He commissioned them to this work.

Can you imagine a Christian faith without the Great Commission? Jesus would have simply comforted those first disciples with the assurance that their sins were forgiven, that death was conquered, and that they would have his eternal presence with them, but he would not have prompted them to do anything more. They would still have an amazing story to tell about the work of God through Jesus Christ but would have no reason to tell it. It would have been a private blessing they reaped for their faithfulness to Jesus during his earthly ministry.

Without the commission, Pentecost might never have happened and the church might never have formed. The disciples would simply have lived as a gracious community, sharing their common joy with each other until each passed into glory, and leaving the world destitute of ever knowing the gospel.

As impossible as that scenario sounds, a great many of our congregations live as if this is what happened. They focus on the people who are already part of the church, without giving much thought about how to go and make disciples of Jesus Christ in the world around them. As Ed Stetzer and Eric Geiger put it, "Christians are not following Christ, and we are making no difference in our neighborhoods, much less the world."[1]

One way we see this is in a lack of evangelism. It is not that the people in our congregations think sharing their faith is unimportant. A 2012 LifeWay Research report found that "80 percent of those who attend church one or more times a month believe they have a personal responsibility to share their faith." However, only "25 percent say they have shared their faith once or twice, and 14 percent have shared three or more times over the last six months."[2] That means 61 percent of Christians have not shared their faith at all in the previous six months. Clearly our beliefs do not drive what most of us do.

Pastors are little different from the laity on this point. Rick Richardson, a professor of evangelism at Wheaton College, has found that a primary reason many lay Christians do not evangelize is because their pastors do not share their faith outside of a church context. Apart from regular meetings that occur at least monthly in which pastors are held accountable for this sort of faith-sharing, personal evangelism for pastors "falls off the map."[3]

If this is how we act as individual Christians, our congregations are sure to follow suit. After all, we are the people who make up our congregations! Even if we think "the church" ought to obey the Great Commission, our local congregations have no capacity to carry out that mandate if we are individually unwilling to do the work. We have nowhere to pass the buck.

This dichotomy of what we believe and what our congregations are equipped to do leads to a variety of problems. Declining

---

1   Ed Stetzer and Eric Geiger, *Transformational Groups: Creating a New Scorecard for Groups* (Nashville: B&H Books, 2014), 21.
2   Jon D. Wilke, "Churchgoers Believe in Sharing Faith, Most Never Do," http://www .lifeway.com/Article/research-survey-sharing-christ-2012.
3   Rick Richardson, "Local Church Culture & Evangelistic Witness, Engaging Senior Leaders (part 2 of 4)," *ReKindle: Engaging in Gospel Conversations*, November 18, 2015, https:// www.youtube.com/watch?v=HDcXzxRneqs.

memberships and offerings are too well known, especially in North American mainline Protestant churches in the early twenty-first century. Other problems are more pervasive such as a weakened voice for morality, justice, and truth in the public square. Over time, this causes a broader cultural disintegration and allows for corrupt structures and values to embed themselves in the minds and hearts of people who hear no call to discipleship from the church.

Just as it would have done no good if Jesus had come to lead a quiet, sinless life that ended with a peaceful death, so it does no good for the world if the church has a large number of congregations that live quietly focused on their own affairs and eventually die peacefully without disturbing anybody. Jesus came to call people to repentance and to become his disciples. The church is commissioned to do the same. To avoid this mission is to fail to be what we are supposed to be.

This text is about creating missional congregations by giving people in those congregations the tactics they need to live out the strategy of the Great Commission. Having grown up in the church and served in local congregations as lay member, youth leader, and pastor, I am convinced that one of the reasons that local congregations do not make disciples is that they simply don't know what they need to do. The call to "go make disciples" is clear enough, but figuring out practices that allow us to obey this call is harder, especially when all the institutional aspects of the local congregation also clamor for our attention.

Missional Congregations
Living into Our Humanity

What does it mean to be a missional congregation? Contrary to what may first come to mind, it is *not* about setting up a new committee or launching new programs, though a congregation may do those things as it lives into being missional. Instead, it is about the nature of the church.

The word *mission* comes from the Latin *missio*, which means "to send." Simply put, a missional congregation is a congregation that is sent. But where is it sent and what is it sent to do? To answer those questions, we must first consider the nature of the God who sends the church. As Craig Ott puts it, "When we speak of the mission of the church . . . we must also explore the ways in which the very *nature* of the church is defined by its relationship to the Triune God, who is a missionary God."[4]

To use Ott's phrase, God is a "missionary God" in two ways. The first is that God is personally active as a missionary. Before God sent anyone else, God sent God. In fact, God has been sending God throughout the history of the world. The Father sent the Spirit to brood over the waters and breathe life into creation. The Father sent the Son to redeem creation from its sin. The Father and Son sent the Holy Spirit to lead people into truth and demonstrate the power of God's coming kingdom.

God is both the sending God and the sent God. God crafts purposes for the benefit of creation and then comes into creation to carry out those purposes.

God does not do this missionary work alone though. This brings us to the second way that God is a missionary God: God commissions those who are part of creation to participate in accomplishing God's purposes.

Initially, God did this through creating humankind, the only creature bearing God's image. Part of what it means to bear the image of God is to be commissioned to carry out the purposes of God. To be human is to be missional! We see this in how God commissioned Adam and Eve to have dominion over the earth, tending the creation and continuing the work of creation through having children. They joined God in the mission of maintaining creation and fostering its sabbath rest with God.

Later, God commissioned the people of Israel to be in mission. Israel would be a light to the nations through its holy living, defined both by the covenant given to Abraham and the Law given through Moses. It would offer the nations a place to recognize the power and majesty of God and ultimately would bring forth a Messiah who would inaugurate God's kingdom on earth.

---

4   Craig Ott, ed., *The Mission of the Church: Five Views in Conversation* (Grand Rapids: Baker, 2016), ix.

Through the community of believers that gathered around Jesus, and the subsequent empowering of those believers by the Holy Spirit, God commissioned a church from every tribe, tongue, and nation to make disciples who would share in that kingdom. They would do this by sharing the good news of what God had done in the life, death, and resurrection of Jesus by baptizing people into the church and by teaching them the ways of Jesus.

To be a missional congregation is to be a local manifestation of the church: a group of people who are sent by God to live according to Jesus' teachings and to invite others to live according to those teachings. This sending is not to anywhere exotic. It is to where we live already.

If you trace this process of God commissioning people to participate in God's mission from creation through the church, being a missional congregation is simply to be part of a group of people reclaiming what it means to be fully human! We are not adding something new to our identity by being missional. Rather, we are returning to what God created us to be: those who tend creation so that it can be at rest with its loving Creator. We simply now understand that this rest comes through Jesus Christ and that we will experience our rest completely when the kingdom of God comes in its fullness.

Mission and Sin

Interwoven through the story of God sending people to be part of God's mission is the story of God dealing with humanity's sin. This explains why God raises up specific groups such as Israel or the church to participate in God's mission. While all humanity is commissioned, God gives people the choice to reject that commission. Those who accept the commission become a part of the missionally oriented groups God has drawn together. Those who reject this commission are sinners, because they are turning away from God and God's purposes.

If someone rejects God's purposes, it does not mean God rejects that person. Rather, that person becomes an object of God's mission. God reaches out to forgive the person's sin and to reconcile the person back to God. God also works to overcome any forces that encourage the person to remain sinful.

Part of being a missional congregation is to confront sin. This involves loving those who sin, so they can be redeemed to their human birthright of being part of God's purposes. It also involves standing against human structures that encourage people to turn from God.

Engaging sin this way is difficult. We offer God's love to those who maybe apathetic, resistant, or even hostile to it. God recognizes this and sets the example for how to undertake this aspect of our mission. As the sent God, the Son of God became incarnate in Jesus of Nazareth, willingly died on the cross to overcome sin, and rose again to show that God's kingdom would ultimately prevail. A missional congregation must likewise expect that it will endure times of sacrifice and hardship, but it has the hope of the resurrection guaranteeing its efforts will be worthwhile when the kingdom comes.

Being a missional congregation, then, is not about specific practices, committees, or programs. It is about our core beliefs concerning God and obeying what God created us—both as humans and as a church—to do. It is about recognizing that we are, as Len Sweet puts it, not just called to make a difference in the world but to be part of God making a different world altogether.[5] It is to participate with God in finishing the good work God began in creation. It is then taking that recognition and living into it, letting the Holy Spirit form us more fully as disciples of Jesus Christ, so we can help others become his disciples.

One Strategy, Many Tactics

In my experience, while most congregations are grateful and even inspired by learning about the missional nature of the church, they get stuck figuring out what to do with that information. How is a congregation supposed to participate in accomplishing God's purposes?

Here's the good news: while there is one mission God has given us, to go make disciples, we have many ways of accomplishing it. Being active in missions doesn't just mean talking to people about Jesus

---

5   Leonard Sweet, plenary address, United Methodist Church School of Congregational Development, Evanston, IL, August 18, 2016.

or working against injustice. It means everything we do to create a disciple-making environment for the world around us. Anything that catches people's attention by demonstrating what the kingdom of God is like, welcomes people to be part of that kingdom, and teaches people how to live as followers of Jesus Christ in that kingdom is a missional activity. Most of this happens in ordinary ways.

Jesus understood the ordinariness of how we live out the call to make disciples. Just the word *go* he used in the Great Commission suggests this. In the Matthew passage, the verb tense in Greek is better translated "as you are going" rather than just "go." Jesus was not commanding his disciples (and us!) to move from one place to another to make disciples, but to make disciples as part of our everyday life—as we are going about our ordinary routines.

And what can we do to make disciples as we move through our daily lives? A brief examination of the five commissioning texts provides multiple activities:

> Teach, baptize (Matthew)
> Preach, perform miraculous signs (Mark)
> Preach to all nations, be witnesses (Luke)
> Be at peace, forgive sins, receive the Holy Spirit, believe (John)
> Be witnesses in Jerusalem, Judea, Samaria, and the ends of the earth (Acts)

There is nothing heroic or superhuman required in these. They are just the regular work of seeking God in our lives and interacting with other people in a way that helps them recognize the presence and power of God—things we are already doing in our congregations.

This should be great news for our local congregations! There is no one activity or technique to master. Rather, we can choose the practices of mission that fit best with who we are and the situations we face.

There is also room to adapt these practices to our congregations. Teaching, for example, might look different for a congregation with a large children's Sunday school from a congregation that is mostly made up of older adults. The tactics are not cookie cutters meant to force congregations to look a specific way or to adopt specific programs. They offer congregations many ways forward as they "go" into mission through their daily lives.

One benefit of this broader array of missional activity is that we can reclaim everything we are already doing—our worship, our education, our music, even our administrative committees—as a way of living into God's purposes for the world. Instead of starting new programs or committees, we can take what we are doing and trust God to breathe the life of mission into it.

The list of activities a congregation can use to live into its missional identity is even larger than what is found in the five commissioning passages. God has commissioned people throughout the Bible to go participate in God's mission. By looking at other passages where this commissioning happens, we can add even more tactics to our plan for making disciples.

This book seeks to help you do just that. It examines passages in the Bible in which the people of God are commissioned to go on God's behalf. Drawing from these, it lays out a several practical suggestions for how congregations can become missional congregations.

Each chapter offers insight into a specific tactic for engaging in mission. These tactics include going into hiding (chap.1), going to places we would rather not go (chap. 2), going into the presence of God (chap. 3), refusing to go away when intimidated (chap. 4), going into exile (chap. 5), going to reconcile with God and others (chap. 6), and going to celebrate life (chap. 7). The final chapter reminds us that where God calls us to go, Jesus has already gone, so we can go with confidence. Congregations can use these chapters to discern how the Holy Spirit might guide them to be missional.

No congregation will be able to undertake all these tactics at all times. Just as in a battle, we must change tactics depending on our situation. This should be encouraging to us! It demonstrates that God understands we cannot always engage in mission the same way, so we are free to adapt to the situations we face. In this way, God is more understanding about mission than most of us who want to keep doing the same thing we have always done, even when it has stopped being effective.

For those uneasy about making this sort of change, remember that the congregation is only changing its procedures or processes of ministry, not changing its core. Its core has always been to participate in accomplishing God's purposes. That is what God created humanity, and specifically the church, to do. The congregation is just finding ways to do what it was always supposed to do.

Congregations like to establish standard operating procedures and stick to them. They are familiar and can even be effective. However, they are rarely flexible. As a result, when we face situations that force us to modify those procedures, we often feel as though we are failing in mission. We think we can succeed only when we are doing a certain activity.

God, however, does not expect us to do the same thing all the time. God understands that we are in an ever-changing world that requires creativity and adaptability. Because of this, God has a bevy of tactics for our congregations to remain missional, regardless of what situation we might face.

Answering Some Questions
What about Growth?

Let me answer a few questions you may have at the outset. The primary one is likely: Will the tactics in this book help our church to grow?

As a congregation participates in God's mission, that congregation likely will grow. After all, if we are making disciples by both baptizing, which means we are bringing new people into a community of faith, and teaching, which means we are providing something meaningful that encourages them to stay, then our congregation ought to grow. In fact, even if we are regularly sending people out of our congregations to be missionaries and church planters (which we should be doing!), statistics show we will continue to grow.[6] Being missional points us in the right direction to increase our congregations in size. That said, *church growth is not the aim of mission*.

---

6   Ed Stetzer and Daniel Im, *Planting Missional Churches: Your Guide to Starting Churches that Multiply* (Nashville: B&H Academic, 2016), 324–25.

For years those of us in the North American context have been conditioned to think of missions as a matter of claiming new people and resources for the kingdom of God. This work should be attended by positive results that mirror success in the marketplace: a large arrow pointing toward the upper right corner of the graph indicating growth in money and membership.

The fact is, not all congregations are poised to engage in this sort of advance, and even when they are, not all will see dramatic increases in numbers. God understands that. We need to understand it, too, and not feel as though we are failing if we are not posting big statistical gains. God wants us to make disciples, and God gives us a variety of ways to do that. So long as we are being faithful in this, we are doing exactly what Jesus commissioned us to do.

We can apply Paul's point about marriage to this concern about growth:

> I want you to be free from anxieties. The unmarried man is anxious about the affairs of the Lord, how to please the Lord; but the married man is anxious about the affairs of the world, how to please his wife, and his interests are divided. And the unmarried woman and the virgin are anxious about the affairs of the Lord, so that they may be holy in body and spirit; but the married woman is anxious about the affairs of the world, how to please her husband. I say this for your own benefit, not to put any restraint upon you, but to promote good order and unhindered devotion to the Lord. (1 Cor 7:32-35)

Paul explained that any human commitment will absorb some of our attention and energy. It is not that those commitments are wrong, but they can steal our focus from God. Even our commitment to demonstrate good growth numbers for our congregation can lead us away from God. Our congregations become idols to us rather than God's instruments for calling people to be disciples!

As Paul wrote elsewhere, "For freedom Christ has set us free. Stand firm, therefore, and do not submit again to a yoke of slavery"

(Gal 5:1). We are freed to take our focus off the numbers, trusting that God will make disciples through us as we faithfully work alongside God. Let's claim our freedom and see what God will do, trusting that God is already ranging through the world to carry out God's own mission and is inviting us along to participate!

In addition, if we want to make a significant difference in the culture around us, we should be less concerned about the number of people in our congregations and more concerned about the total number of disciples of Jesus Christ in the region our congregations serve. If we focus on this total number of disciples, it opens the door to new ways of doing mission that move us outside our congregations. The first is by allowing us to partner with other congregations to make a collective missional impact in a region, rather than each of our congregations trying to go it alone. Second, it might convince our congregation to get pregnant! A pregnant congregation is one that sends out people to plant new congregations. Just like with biological pregnancies, congregations should be mature and healthy but then focus their resources and energy to launch new life into the world. Such a plan may mean smaller congregations in the end, but many more disciples of Jesus Christ influencing the local culture. This is the pattern of ministry John Wesley used to "spread scriptural holiness" across England, Scotland, Ireland, and Wales.

Are Other Parts of the Bible Equal to the Great Commission?

In this book we will be looking at several passages where God sends God's people on mission, using all of them to discern tactics for our congregations to be in mission. But shouldn't the Great Commission take precedence since it was the final command of Jesus? Is it appropriate to lay it beside several other passages that come from both Old and New Testaments?

I do believe that the Great Commission has a unique place in how the church should understand itself. Through it Jesus told the church that its mission is to make disciples. However, the logic of the entire Bible is missional. God sent Adam, Noah, Abraham, and the kings and prophets of Israel to "go" as part of God's divine mission—just as surely as God sent Jesus, the apostles, and us.

In this sense, the Great Commission is the capstone of God's involvement in mission throughout human history, calling anyone who hears and responds to join in the missional work of making disciples. It tells us broadly how to do this: by going and baptizing and teaching, but it is not meant to be a comprehensive list of everything we do in mission. The other passages in which God commissions people provide us with additional insight into how we can live into that mission.

In fact, even the approach I've chosen of looking at passages that describe people going somewhere by God's order does not create an exhaustive list of possible missional practices. There are certainly additional tactics available for congregations to be missional. I encourage you and your congregation to search the Bible for these. Looking at these passages shows us there is a wide range of activities we can use to be in mission, some even running counter to what we often think of as mission. This means we need to keep an open mind as we explore these tactics.

One reason there are so many unexpected missional practices is that congregations can find themselves in a wide variety of situations. We are not always on an even keel with resources available. There are times when a congregation might face persecution or has to confront a sudden need in the community where it serves. It can be easy in the face of these situations for the congregation to feel unequipped because it is outside of its standard ways of being in mission. These tactics provide us with insight into how we can stay missional in the midst of changing situations.

Are Programming and Character Both Important?

Some of these tactics deal with programming we can enact, but some are with our character as a congregation. Why is that?

It is not enough only to engage in specific practices. We need to allow God to form us so we are missional. Remember, to be missional means to believe that God is active in bringing about God's purposes in the world and that we are joining God in this work. Congregations should be intentional about being formed by this belief even as they go to those who are outside their walls. Put another way, if God calls us to make disciples, we should first allow God to make us disciples.

Part of this formation is moving beyond thinking about congregations as entities that only exist on Sunday mornings. The commission of Christ does not expire once Sunday worship is over! The people in the congregation need to reimagine themselves as missionaries who gather weekly in their missionary outpost, but whose primary work is to be in relationship with those outside that outpost throughout the week.

This also means that the tactics in this book are not exclusive of each other. While not all the tactics are appropriate to all situations, there is no reason that a congregation could not engage in several of these tactics at the same time. For example, a congregation could seek the face of God while standing firm in the face of an injustice. Also, since congregations are made up of multiple people, some people within a congregation could employ one tactic while other people employed another. The tactics can shift to accommodate who is available and what those people's gifts and passions are.

Why the Emphasis on Local Congregations?

Much of the missional church literature today focuses on the creation of movements and new church starts. This is very helpful as we imagine what it means to be a missional church in the new cultural context of North America. However, in this book I want to consider how local congregations that already exist can become missional.

Why this emphasis on existing local congregations? In part, it is because I love the local congregation. I have dedicated much of my life to living and serving in local congregations, and in the periods of my life when I have not had a congregation to call my own, I have felt that loss. I truly believe the local congregation is where God meets people, forms a community, and transforms lives. The congregation is more than the sum of its individual members. It is a holy union of people with Christ and each other that has almost limitless possibilities for how it can bless the world.

The local congregation does not just bless the world generically. It is the primary way people can participate in the mission of God. *The Book of Discipline of The United Methodist Church* explains this, stating that the purpose of the church is "to make disciples of Jesus Christ for the transformation of the world," and that "local churches provide the most significant arena through which disciple making occurs."[7] If we do not equip our congregations to engage in God's mission, we hamstring the primary means God created to carry out that mission!

I also want to focus on established local congregations because I know how hard it is, especially for smaller and struggling congregations, to feel they can go and be effective witnesses for Jesus Christ. My first experience as a solo pastor was of a thirty-two-member congregation that was considering whether to close the doors when I arrived. The tight budget, small number of people, and low morale demanded something different to guide us from the various success stories we read about in evangelism and mission literature.

Most of the role-model ministries are out of touch with the realities that small, established congregations face. The role models all seem to be new church starts that are unbelievably effective at welcoming new people, or megachurches dripping with resources, or specialized Christian communities and parachurch organizations that make a remarkable difference in their political, economic, and social contexts. Even though some of these role models started as small, struggling congregations, their current burgeoning success makes it difficult for leaders of established congregations to connect with them.

Established congregations can easily slip into despair when these are the only examples they have for how to be missional. They know they do not have the resources that the role models have in terms of expertise, energy, money, or people. They also feel guilty because they are not doing more. The result is that they often become demoralized, which leads either to doing nothing or to

---

7   *The Book of Discipline of The United Methodist Church 2012* (Nashville: The United Methodist Publishing House, 2013), ¶120.

rallying people around various programs in hopes that something will work. As Paul Borthwick in *Great Commission, Great Compassion* observed, "Guilt offers no cure; it only paralyzes us or stirs us to impulsive action."[8]

I know this unhappy place. I faced it when I served my small congregation. Having endured decline after a series of traumatic events, the congregation was not ready to step into missional outreach. For over a year, we needed to work on reestablishing trust within the congregation. Even when we had built that trust, most of our resources were needed to run the basic operations of the congregation and to deal with long overdue maintenance on the building. It was only after four years that the congregation was ready for a bigger vision of how to engage in mission beyond itself.

During these four years, we were consistently reminded of our tiny status by two congregations of the same denomination in our town that each had several hundred people attending worship. Even when we took major strides for our little congregation, what we did seemed insignificant in the shadow of these far bigger congregations. Adding further discouragement, we were shamed by the denomination's quarterly giving report that showed we were well behind in paying our denominational obligations.

As un-missional as those four years may have seemed, let me encourage those of you in similar situations with this critical insight I gained: *time spent healing is not time wasted*. Many established congregations have long festering wounds that need healing. Just as our physical bodies are hampered in being active when we are injured, so a local body of Christ will be hampered in being a faithful witness if there are serious fractures within it. Healing an established congregation may not be glamorous, but it is essential if the people are hurt. By the same token, just as most physical injuries do not sideline us from all activity, focusing on healing a congregation does not make it impossible for us to engage in missional work. There are almost always ways we can continue to go and make disciples.

---

8   Paul Borthwick. *Great Commission, Great Compassion: Following Jesus and Loving the World* (Downers Grove, IL: InterVarsity Press), 99.

I am grateful that my little congregation did not give up during those four years of healing. By discerning our strengths and working from them, we were able to engage in missions that required minimal personnel and finances. For example, we provided a place for an eclectic set of about thirty kids from the local high school to hang out and talk about faith, helped two teenage girls to stop cutting themselves, and built an inexpensive stage with volunteer labor on land we owned to provide small concerts for the neighborhood.

While we were nowhere near being the kind of successful congregation that we read about in books or heard lauded by church officials, we used what little we had to create a space where we could make disciples. Like the steward from the parable who only received one talent, meaning he could do far less than the stewards who received two or five, we did not have much, but we still could make use of what little we had. Even if we did not have attention-getting results and we continued to be beleaguered by internal strife, facilities problems, limited finances, and tension with the denomination, we could still follow Paul's admonition, "So let us not grow weary in doing what is right, for we will reap at harvest time, if we do not give up" (Gal 6:9).

As an encouragement to others who know the struggles of leading an established congregation, what I want to suggest is that we need both a more focused understanding of the Great Commission and a broader view of the tactics God gives us to carry out that mission. The Great Commission is not about becoming a remarkable success story but about going to make disciples of Jesus Christ. As focused as that mission is, the tactics are infinite. There are many activities that help us do this work, and they are all provided as a gift from God.

Does Being Missional Mean Becoming Radical?

In this book I deal with some touchy social issues, such as race and privilege. Is that necessary to be missional? It makes it sound like being missional requires us to be social radicals.

Our primary goal as a missional congregation is to make disciples of Jesus Christ, no more and no less. What does it look like to be a disciple of Jesus Christ? It looks like someone who strives to obey the two greatest commandments: to love God and to love neighbor.

This love should be visible on an individual level, with individual Christians treating other individuals with love by caring for their needs, forgiving them, and acknowledging their dignity as human beings. It should also be visible on a corporate level. If we truly love people, we will also consider the larger contexts in which they live. What are the cultural values that affect them? How do they relate to the social, economic, and political structures around them? Where can they feel comfortable gathering?

As we consider these questions, we find that many people live in situations that are broken, either because they are harmed by the values and structures around them or because those values and structures have taught them to be negligent toward their neighbors. Either way, to make disciples is to work for love in these situations. This requires working to transform the structures that hurt people or that encourage some people to neglect their neighbors.

This is not to suggest that we become preoccupied with cultural, social, political, or economic agendas. It is to say that we cannot love our neighbors well or nurture people into the teachings of Jesus Christ fully if we ignore these aspects of people's lives. Being a disciple does not mean being nice to other people one-on-one, but working to demonstrate and welcome people into God's redemptive love in as many ways as possible. In doing this, it will be almost impossible for us to avoid engaging with complicated social ills.

In this book, I look at how this call to discipleship makes the people in a white church rethink their assumptions and change how they relate to the Hispanics who live in the same town. I deal with a white congregation because I know that context well, having grown up and served in white congregations. I chose to have this congregation interact with Hispanics because Hispanics now compose the largest nonwhite segment of the American population. I also deal with how a more conservative, largely older congregation relates to a group of more progressive young adults. I include this because generational fault lines are often very real in congregations, leading to stalemates and hurt feelings. I wanted to offer ideas for how different age groups could collaborate toward a common mission.

I realize that the relationships among these groups in the book are a bit contrived at times. They could take many other forms in different contexts and could spawn other missional solutions. I present these not to provide the only missional ways forward but to explore these relationships from the perspective of a congregation seeking to be missional. Hopefully, this can fire your imagination for how to make disciples holistically in your situation.

I am also aware that there are more divisions than just ethnic/racial and generational ones. There are immigrant congregations struggling to relate to the mainstream culture of their adopted country, regions where denominational divides still run deep, and towns where classism separates the poor from the rich even though they are all the same race and ethnicity. The list could go on. Sadly, we as humans divide ourselves in as many ways as we have learned to categorize ourselves. Your congregation may face a different set of unloving structures and attitudes, but the same logic of seeking to make disciples by enacting love in those situations holds firm.

Introducing First Church

To make this book more accessible and applicable to local congregations, woven throughout our examination of the various Bible passages is the story of First Church. Drawn loosely from my own observations of a variety of congregations, First Church provides descriptions of how engaging in various missional tactics might play out for a local congregation. I readily admit that the story I unfold around First Church is fictional and that I sometimes use convenient plot devices to bring out the different tactics I want to discuss. That said, I have worked to make First Church reasonably realistic. There are very few situations in which I place First Church that are not based on actual situations of congregations and pastors.

First Church is a mainline congregation that is nearly one hundred years old. Located in a quiet neighborhood of a small town, First Church was never large. At its height, one hundred people might have worshiped on a Sunday. In more recent years the stagnant demographics in the town, combined with the aging of the congregation and the fewer children and grandchildren coming to church, has led to worship attendance that can fluctuate between sixty to eighty on an average Sunday. Even a hint of bad weather sends the attendance plummeting (whether or not a storm ever develops!).

First Church is sustained by its most loyal congregants. About twenty people have been attending for most of their adult lives, and they give generously. They are not wealthy people, but it is enough for the church to maintain a consistent annual budget of around $65,000. The bulk of that goes to pay the pastor with the rest covering the costs of maintenance and some programming. Those same people are mostly retired, so they also give generously of their time and expertise. This means the pastor has help in running the day-to-day operations, such as printing the bulletins and keeping the grounds.

The people of First Church are loving to one another. The core folks have been together long enough that they have shared the good and the bad, including births, weddings, baptisms, illnesses, and funerals. They have had their fallings-out at times, but they have always stuck together. Even with larger, more active churches being planted within easy driving distance from First Church's building, this group is committed to seeing First Church remain solid.

By the same token, the congregation is getting grayer and a little more tired every year. The older folks are heard to say, half-jokingly, that they are ready to retire from helping run so much of the church. Committee meetings and workdays absorb a lot of time. The half dozen younger families are turned to more frequently than ever to keep programs going, especially programs for children.

The pastors at First Church have been hard workers over the years, but aside from a lengthy pastorate a decade ago, most pastors do not stay long. They come, are loved, and often return that love but move on within three or four years to more promising congregations. The people care for their pastors, but the steady coming and going of those pastors has left them yearning for stability.

The congregation is not entirely inward looking. They have their annual fall festival and host an ecumenical prayer breakfast once a month that even has had local town officials attend it. They also run an annual vacation Bible school. Recently, there was enough interest from the young families to develop a children's choir and to pay for a part-time musician to direct it. The children and parents have enjoyed his energy and expertise so much that the choir has grown as community parents have begun bringing their children to participate in it.

Even with all this, the people of First Church feel like they are not making much of a difference. They know they are called to something more than just "doing church," but they are not certain what. It requires so much of their effort just to keep the usual church activities going (Sunday worship, Sunday school and Bible studies, music program, and various administrative committees) that they have little time or energy to imagine what being a missional congregation might mean. When they hear occasional talks about it from denominational officials, they just sigh and think about how much extra work it would take in addition to what they already do. After all, isn't becoming missional a matter of establishing a new mission committee and new missional programs? Who has time for that? Missions seem like something tacked on to the regular work of a congregation. If it were essential to the life of the congregation, the congregation wouldn't have survived as long as it has doing the same thing it has always done, right?

What the people of First Church don't know is that they are in store for a roller coaster ride that will prompt them to become more missional. As with many congregations (and even denominations), this will not happen because they are seeking to be missional but because of desperation. Faced with serious struggles, the leadership of First Church will make critical decisions about what they believe and how they will live out those beliefs. Based on the ways they recognize God in these situations, they will be formed into God's mission.

A Word of Encouragement

In one of his best-known sonnets, often entitled "On His Blindness," the seventeenth-century Anglican priest John Donne explained how God welcomed and employed all people regardless of their ability. He wrote the poem as he struggled with going blind, wondering what use he would be to God without his vision. The conclusion of the poem spoke not only to his situation but also to the situation of many congregations today that are fearful of their small stature and diminishing resources:

> God doth not need
> Either man's work or his own gifts; who best
> Bear his mild yoke, they serve him best. His state
> Is kingly. Thousands at his bidding speed
> And post o'er land and ocean without rest:
> They also serve who only stand and wait.

Whether we are those who can "post o'er land and ocean without rest" or we are those who "only stand and wait," we are still able to be missional. We are still God's people, redeemed by Jesus Christ, baptized into the Holy Spirit, and commissioned to make disciples. We are anointed and strengthened for this work, and God has tactics available to help us accomplish it. That those tactics do not fit with our cultural expectations of success does not matter. What matters is that we have served as best we can. And, according to the parable of the talents, God has the same welcome for all Christians who have been faithful whether they were given much or little: "Well done, thou good and faithful servant!"

My hope for this book is that it will encourage and equip congregations, especially existing mainline congregations. For congregations that feel as though they are left behind in being able to live out the Great Commission, I pray this book will help you see how to be missional without having to become a marketplace success story. For congregations bewildered by what to do because they are dealing with issues that are outside of how they have been used to operating, I pray these tactics will give you a foothold from which to engage those issues while staying in mission. For all congregations, I hope this book provides a way to revisit and reclaim the Great Commission with creativity, excitement, and intentionality.

RETREAT FORWARD

Genesis 7:1-4
Proverbs 28:12, 28

"Retreat!"

That is not a sound that we want to hear if we are fighting in a battle. To retreat is to disengage and run back to safety. It is associated with failure and loss. The winners don't retreat; they advance boldly and lay claim to the disputed territory. They raise their banners and spread the news that they are victorious. Only the conquered and oppressed retreat, giving up the battle in hopes of living another day.

The notion of retreating makes just as little sense in reference to obeying the Great Commission. How can we retreat if we want to be witnesses before all nations? We must press forward, shrugging aside the danger we face, and make disciples. I have even known church groups and evangelists to rename "retreats" (women's retreats, youth retreats, and so on), calling them "advances" so that the people on them do not think their time away with the church suggests they are being defeated.

The Gospels and the book of Acts seem to bear this out. They are full of stories about Jesus and the earliest Christians pressing ahead in the face of terrible opposition. Jesus shrugs off warnings that Herod is after him (Luke 13:31-32) and openly criticizes the Pharisees and teachers of the Law (Luke 11). Peter and John endure their first persecution and refuse to quit speaking in the name of Jesus

(Acts 4:18-21). Paul receives several messages cautioning him against returning to Jerusalem and goes anyway (Acts 21:12-14). It seems that mission happens by pushing forward in the face of severe opposition.

Yet to view Jesus and the early church only through these passages is to bypass several places where their forward motion comes not from pressing ahead but from retreating. Neither Jesus nor the early church was always in the limelight, preaching and performing miracles. There are several times they drew away in order to pray:

- After his first major public success healing and preaching in Galilee, Jesus went to a deserted place to pray (Luke 4:42). Retreating to be alone and pray was a common practice for Jesus (Luke 5:16).
- Following the Ascension the few followers of Jesus gathered in the upper room where they had met the risen Lord to pray and stay in fellowship apart from any public ministry until the Holy Spirit descended on the Day of Pentecost (Acts 1:12-14, 2:1).
- After the persecution of Peter and John, the followers of Jesus again gathered in private to pray (Acts 4:23-24). This was a common practice for the church in times when it faced dangerous opposition.

Being in mission includes retreating so we can exit the public eye and dedicate ourselves to prayer. When we retreat to pray, it is not a failure of mission but a way of engaging in mission that focuses on seeking the supernatural provision and protection of God.

There are times when retreat and prayer are the wisest tactical moves that congregations can make to carry out the larger strategy of making disciples. These are times when the congregation needs to re-center on God's mission and on God's presence alongside them as they participate in that mission. During these times, congregations can be reminded of their

- faith that God is active in the world;
- faith that the power of God has overcome the powers of evil;

- faith that our human effort is not the driving power to accomplish God's will;
- faith that God listens to and acts through prayer;
- belief that they are part of God's mission, not that God is part of their mission.

To live in this faith is to live in the realm of tremendous possibility. For if we have the faith of a mustard seed, Jesus said that is enough for God to accomplish amazing things through us (Matt 17:20; Luke 17:6).

Two passages, Genesis 7:1-4 and Proverbs 28:12, 28, help us better understand what retreating to pray looks like. The Genesis passage describes God commanding Noah and his family to go into the ark. From Proverbs we learn that the righteous must go into hiding when there is a strong presence of evil in leadership.

First Church's Struggles

First Church was facing a difficult time. During an exceptionally cold and snowy winter, it had to cancel Sunday services three times. The services it did hold had been more lightly attended than usual, including on Christmas Eve. In addition to the disappointment people in the congregation felt from not being able to gather and celebrate with each other, another pressing issue arose. Since people were not present to put their offerings in the plate, giving was down. Without a substantial Christmas Eve offering, which the congregation always counted on to cover its usual end-of-year budget gap, the congregation had closed the year in the red. This was compounded by the small offering income during January and February.

The finance committee had cut back every expenditure it could to make ends meet. This included freezing the pastor's salary, not reimbursing people who had purchased things for the church, holding off on buying new curriculum and materials for the Sunday school, and only paying the most pressing bills.

To top it off, as the cold weather persisted into March, the people arrived one Sunday morning to find the sanctuary uncomfortably cold. Quick investigation discovered that the boiler had given out, and at least two pipes had burst because of the freezing temperatures overnight. The costs for replacing the boiler and the pipes would be far more than the congregation had in its already strained operating funds and would even extend beyond the "rainy day" fund the church had set aside for emergencies.

What were the people of First Church to do? Would their strained financial and maintenance situation mean that they must give up any hope of being missional? Is their only option to turn within themselves and focus on survival?

Go into the Ark: God's Provision

> Then the LORD said to Noah, "Go into the ark, you and all your household, for I have seen that you alone are righteous before me in this generation. Take with you seven pairs of all clean animals, the male and its mate; and a pair of the animals that are not clean, the male and its mate; and seven pairs of the birds of the air also, male and female, to keep their kind alive on the face of all the earth. For in seven days I will send rain on the earth for forty days and forty nights; and every living thing that I have made I will blot out from the face of the ground." (Gen 7:1-4)

The move toward survival is natural enough, and it is something that many congregations around North America have adopted. When the only options are to live or die, we instinctively focus all our energy on fighting to live. In such cases, it seems that mission is no longer in the picture. Or, at least, mission must be deferred. We can get back to participating in God's purposes once we have secured our own health and well-being.

This seems logical, but it is a mistake. The church is never in a life and death situation where its only option is to turn within itself without regard for mission. This is because the nature of the church is to be missional. Just as God cannot avoid being both the Sender and the Sent One, the church can never be anything but sent to make disciples. While congregations may have to retreat from public ministry for a while because of internal difficulties, they are still missional, and they can continue to make disciples by witnessing to the presence and power of God in the world. One of the ways they can maintain this witness while retreating is by demonstrating their reliance on the provision of God. This is a countercultural move. Rather than being defined by the bottom line, the church becomes defined by faith.

This call to retreat so that we can rely on God's provision comes through in the story of Noah. In the passage from Genesis 7, God commands Noah and his family to go into the ark along with all the animals. The ark is God's provision to survive the flood. To retreat from the overwhelming disaster happening outside the ark is not an act of cowardice; it is an act of obedience that allows Noah and company to survive a situation they never could have withstood on their own.

Entering the ark was more than just a matter of saving themselves though. Notice the reason God sends both the people and the animals into the ark: "to keep their kind alive on the face of all the earth" (Gen 7:3). God does not simply desire the people on the ark to survive. God calls the people to retreat into the ark to provide a way for life to persist after the flood.

The logic of this retreat into God's provision is missional! By providing for Noah, his family, and the animals, God is also calling Noah, his family, and the animals to participate in God's purpose of bringing about a renewed creation from the floodwaters. Only by retreating to the ark could Noah and the others be effective missionaries for God in this way.

Of course, neither Noah, his family, nor the animals would likely have seen this larger picture at the time. They would have just known God had provided the ark, and they were able to get on board and survive in a time of crisis. Still, by obeying the call to retreat instead of trying to fight the floodwaters on their own, they not only found that God had given them what they needed to survive but also found they would be able to carry on the missionary call to fill the world and have dominion over it.

Perhaps more startlingly, God even calls Noah and his family away from reaching out to those in need during the flood. Once the waters had begun to rise, it seems likely that Noah and his family could have found numerous potential converts who would have gladly lived according to God's ways and become "members" on board the ark. Yet God "shut [them] in" (Gen 7:16) when the rain began to fall, keeping them from heading out to recruit these folks.

Again, this has to do with being part of God's larger purposes. God's purpose was not just to add a few—or even a few hundred—new people to the ark. God's purpose was to redeem the earth and all the types of creatures on it, including the human species. Only retreating to rely on God would allow Noah and his family to be part of this larger purpose. Human-generated efforts to gather new passengers for the ark would have strained the support system God provided to carry out the purpose of purifying and redeeming all creation through the flood.

The idea that we retreat from our daily routines, our public spaces, or our own efforts so we might be blessed by God's provision and used by God to breathe life into creation is a consistent refrain throughout the Bible. God's call for Noah to go into the ark is a dramatic example of it, but it is most persistently present in the command to keep the Sabbath.

I remember hearing debates when I was growing up as to whether it was acceptable to get your tires rotated or go out to eat on Sunday since doing so would force other people to work. This misses the point of the Sabbath, just as Noah trying to recruit more passengers for the ark would have missed the point of God's desire to redeem all of creation through the flood.

The logic of the Sabbath is to retreat from our routines and to depend upon God's provision. This point is clear in the call for the weekly Sabbath found in Exodus 20:8-11:

> Remember the sabbath day, and keep it holy. Six days you shall labor and do all your work. But the seventh day is a sabbath to the LORD your God; you shall not do any work—you, your son or your daughter, your male or female slave, your livestock, or the alien resident in your towns. For in six days the LORD made heaven and earth, the sea, and all that is in them, but rested the seventh day; therefore the LORD blessed the sabbath day and consecrated it.

The idea is that we rest from our labors so we can dedicate our time and energy to remembering the provision of God. In addition to our resting, we invite all our household, including any animals we own, to retreat from their daily labors so they can also recognize the provision of God as the Creator of all things.

By both honoring God for the provisions we receive, and helping others pause to recognize God's provision for their lives, we are engaged in mission. We are witnessing to our belief in the One who creates, sustains, and nurtures us. We are also showing that we trust God's provision more than we trust our efforts to sustain ourselves.

Deuteronomy 5:15 adds another reason for retreating into the Sabbath: it reminds us not only of God's provision in creation but of God's provision of redemption. After enjoining the Israelites to rest, it says, "Remember that you were a slave in the land of Egypt, and the LORD your God brought you out from there with a mighty hand and an outstretched arm; therefore the LORD your God commanded you to keep the sabbath day." The call is to be missional in witnessing to God's redemptive work by retreating from our daily activities. Just as the Israelites rested from their bondage when God set them free from Egypt, so we rest now to remember how God has set us free from the power of sin and death through Jesus Christ.

Consider the implications of this practice for making disciples. If we took missional retreating as a serious discipline, we would provide a powerful witness for upcoming generations, teaching children from early on that they are a part of something bigger than what they can generate by dint of human ingenuity and effort. We could show them that withdrawing is not weakness but is an act of faith by relying on God's strength.[1]

How we operate in congregations would also change. Our first instinct would be to seek solutions from God's power before turning to what we could produce with our own hands. Would not this

---

1   Walter Brueggemann refers to this sort of activity as "counter nurture," a way of evangelizing our children that immerses them in virtues and values that run counter to the cultural values that would otherwise form them. Walter Brueggemann, *Biblical Perspectives on Evangelism* (Nashville: Abingdon, 1993), 98.

approach to dealing with our congregations' struggles shape the Christians within our congregations? As they became aware of God's presence and power in the congregation's business, they would be equipped to tell concrete stories of God's miraculous provision to a skeptical world. They would not need to defend these stories with philosophical or historical arguments. They would know these stories from firsthand experience.

Our congregations would also have a missional witness that would spread beyond our individual members and households. They would become powerful reminders of a different way of life. This is why, in Exodus 23:13, God follows the command to rest on the Sabbath with the exhortation for the people to "be attentive to all that I have said to you. Do not invoke the names of other gods; do not let them be heard on your lips."

Just like the Israelites' faith in God made them stand out from the peoples around them who believed in multiple gods, the kind of retreating the Sabbath calls us to do in order to know God's provision runs contrary to the logic of how the world around us operates. The world's economies are built on the notion of competing for scarce resources. In such a system, pulling back from competition and relying on the supernatural provision of God does not make sense. It is ludicrous and puts those who do not compete in danger of having nothing. Yet, in the times we are called on to obey it, it is profoundly missional. By retreating, we can demonstrate how God provides for those who are faithfully committed to God's purposes. We can show how living as disciples of Jesus is better than being disciples of the marketplace.

So how did First Church weather its financial and maintenance crises? The pastor called together the leadership of the congregation and laid out the situation, opening the floor for possible solutions. There were several suggestions for how to raise money, including bake sales, an emergency appeal to the membership, and seeking a loan. As the conversation continued in this vein, one of the leaders said, "I remember when we invited the pastor from Haiti to speak to us a couple years ago. He mentioned that they often did not know how they would raise the money they needed for even basic necessities. In those times, he and his team would pray and fast, turning their needs over to God. He said that every time they had done that, the funds they needed were provided. I know it might seem a little absurd, but maybe we can commit to praying for the rest of the week and fasting on one day about our situation. Maybe God will provide for us the way God has provided for the churches in Haiti."

"That's true," another leader responded, "but the Haitian pastor didn't just pray for money. He prayed with a larger vision in mind for how God would bless the community. It was a vision for what he believed God wanted to do, not just for what the pastor or church wanted to do."

The leadership of the church, including the pastor, felt the appropriateness of this call to articulate their vision for what God wanted to do through First Church and then to rely on God. This shifted the conversation. They began to dream about God's desires for their neighborhood and beyond, thinking of how First Church could participate in these things. They saw a missional opportunity before them rather than a stark choice between life and death.

At the same time, they did not want to fall into wishful thinking in the face of such an overwhelming and immediate need. In the end, the group decided to commit to the prayer and fasting while also implementing some of the fund-raising ideas that would be relatively quick and easy to accomplish. The pastor sent out a letter to the congregation that shared the financial needs First Church had, couched in the language of the new vision the leaders had developed; the ladies organized a sub sandwich sale; and the trustees put in some immediate, temporary fixes to keep the other pipes from freezing.

A week later, the congregation witnessed several amazing things. First, in response to the pastor's letter, the people not only recognized they had missed several offerings by not attending services and made up those gifts, but many said they had felt prompted to provide the offerings "with interest." They explained that they were inspired to do this because of the exciting way the letter was written. They were not just meeting an obligation; they were becoming part of the movement of God in the community. The result was more than enough to cover the budget deficit.

This excitement led to the congregation members chatting with their neighbors about what First Church was doing and hoped to do. These were not formal conversations, just natural discussions as friends visited with one another. Not long afterward, the pastor had a visitor come to the church. The owner of a local fuel oil company had heard about the situation from his neighbors. He had been a member of First Church as a child more than fifty years before and had always appreciated the start he had gotten there. He came with a sizable check in hand, saying that his accountants had told him he needed to lower his taxable income for that quarter. The man felt like the congregation was the right place to donate the money. In addition, he was willing to provide a discount on the cost and labor for replacing the boiler.

Of course, not every situation will turn out like this one (although the above story is based on a composite of actual events from my own ministry, including the unexpected visit from the owner of the fuel company!). What it does demonstrate is that retreating to where we are dependent on the provision of God can be a missional act that inspires people to deeper discipleship both inside and outside of a congregation.

Go into Hiding: God's Protection

> When the righteous triumph, there is great glory,
>> but when the wicked prevail, people go into hiding.
> When the wicked prevail, people go into hiding;
>> but when they perish, the righteous increase. (Prov 28:12, 28)

There are other reasons for retreating beyond the need to find God's provisions. While these passages from Proverbs are not commands, we learn that sometimes we need to retreat because we are in danger. Again, this is not cowardice or weakness. It is recognizing that God's protection is far greater than any defense we can mount. It is also a witness to the world that we will not resort to violence even when we are attacked.

The pastor at First Church was starting to breathe easier as the spring moved along and the financial situation became a memory. Pondering the results of prayer and fasting, as well as the increased enthusiasm in the congregation, the last thing he expected was that something would go wrong now. That's why he was so shaken when he arrived at the office one morning to be greeted by a police officer. The officer said he was there to investigate an allegation of sexual abuse perpetrated by a member of the church staff.

Several months earlier, First Church had hired a musician to direct the children's choir. The musician was energetic and talented, even attracting some children from the neighborhood to join the choir. One evening, the musician had the opportunity to be alone with a neighborhood child. During that time, the abuse took place. The child reported what occurred to his mother, and the mother called the police. The mother, as it turned out, was the law clerk to one of the best-known lawyers in town. Hurt by what had happened to her son, the mother explored not only criminal charges against the musician but a lawsuit against the church.

The local media quickly descended on First Church to question how the congregation could have been so careless as to allow something like this to happen. Rumors began to spread that parents had thought there was something inappropriate about the musician for a long time, and they were shocked that the congregation had never taken steps to deal with it before this terrible occurrence. Some, pointing to the recent financial windfall that the congregation had experienced, suggested that the church was just interested in money and would put up with anything to attract more people and more dollars.

Humiliated and ashamed, the people in the congregation did not know what to do. It seemed that they had no good answer to the situation. Under the threat of a lawsuit and disgraced in the eyes of the community, it seemed that all they could do was either fight back by pointing out the pettiness and flaws in the vicious comments people were making about them or just ignore it all and hope it went away. Neither seemed like a good choice.

The late John Howard Yoder, a Mennonite ethicist who is best known for his pacifism, was often asked what he would do if faced with someone who was threatening to kill or injure his loved ones. Would he harm the person despite his pacifism? His answer was that the question was invalid. From his perspective, there is almost always a more creative way to respond than just to kill or be killed. He claimed that of all people, Christians should believe there is another way since they can rely on the supernatural power of God to intervene.[2]

Whether we agree with Yoder's pacifism, his argument about finding a more creative response based on the presence and power of God is helpful. Retreating to hide in the face of danger is a tactic we can understand in this light. It is not an act of weakness, but an act of trust. It is opening the door for God to act as our Protector. This frees us from having to protect ourselves and from engaging in the kind of violent competition that would run counter to our mission of making disciples who obey the teachings of Jesus.

The Bible is full of examples of those who have retreated as an act of mission. David is consistently described as hiding from Saul. Why would the man who fought so valiantly against Goliath and the Philistines and was anointed to be the new king of Israel retreat before Saul and Saul's forces?

David believed that it was wrong for him or his men to raise their hands against the "LORD's anointed." In both 1 Samuel 24 and 26, David is given the opportunity to kill Saul quickly and easily. In both cases, he refused. He chose a life of retreating from Saul because he had a vision of God's bigger purpose for anointing someone as king. The anointed king was to be God's standard-bearer on earth, witnessing to the presence and power of God before both the people of Israel and the nations of the world. For David to have defended himself violently against Saul would have been to dishonor both God and the kingship. It was worth it to David to live for years in hiding rather than to break his witness to the people of Israel.

While retreating to hide from danger, David relied upon God for protection. He also understood that he was participating in God's mission. Some of the psalms attributed to David make both these points, including David's cry for protection and how David will be a missionary by allowing others to see how God has protected him:

---

2   John Howard Yoder, *What Would You Do?* (Scottdale, PA: Herald Press, 1983), 26–42.

- Psalm 59:1, 16: "Deliver me from my enemies, O my God; protect me from those who rise up against me. . . . I will sing of your might; I will sing aloud of your steadfast love in the morning. For you have been a fortress for me and a refuge in the day of my distress."
- Psalm 61:3-4, 8: "For you are my refuge, a strong tower against the enemy. Let me abide in your tent forever, find refuge under the shelter of your wings. . . . So I will always sing praises to your name, as I pay my vows day after day."
- Psalm 64:1, 9: "Hear my voice, O God, in my complaint; preserve my life from the dread enemy. . . . Then everyone will fear; they will tell what God has brought about, and ponder what he has done."

In each case, David cries out for God to hide him from those who would do him harm and concludes with an assurance that people will come to know the gracious power of God because of God's care for the faithful. This contrasts with the terrible fate of those who trust in something other than God. Psalm 16:4 reminds us, "Those who choose another god multiply their sorrows," and Psalm 20:7-8 declares, "Some take pride in chariots, and some in horses, but our pride is in the name of the LORD our God. They will collapse and fall, but we shall rise and stand upright."

In this way, the protection of God is a witness to both the righteous and the persecutors. The righteous can praise God for being faithful to the one who is in hiding. The persecutors are challenged to acknowledge that God is more powerful than they are and is caring for the righteous.

For a congregation to be missional as it goes into hiding, it must remain open to seeing the power of God. To do this, it should expect to learn two things: how to be patient and how to praise. Patience is necessary because God's deliverance does not always come immediately, nor does it always come without cost to the church. The martyrs are evidence of this. God's supernatural power may grant a congregation the ability to persevere against the harm that they experience rather than ending the persecution immediately. This perseverance may last for a long time.

Prayer is an essential act in the midst of this patience, including prayers of praise. Praise is not wishful thinking but a practice of hope. It claims God's power and control are supreme even when the immediate situation does not appear to support that belief. It also solidifies our identity as those who trust God even when our immediate struggles suggest we should put our trust elsewhere to escape from the danger we face. In this sense, praise is one of the most powerful ways we can speak in faith. This idea is explored further in chapter 7.

Engaging in praise is especially important for a congregation, because it gives the people an opportunity to make use of an alternative vocabulary for talking about their struggles. Rather than speaking in terms of competing against those who are persecuting it, it allows the congregation to speak in terms of God's abiding presence and purposes. Everything else falls under this, including the persecutors. This is better than faith becoming subservient to human agendas and rivalries. There are plenty of people who claim God as a mascot supporting their cause, but the missional congregation speaks of God as sovereign over all.

Equipped with this patience and a worldview defined by praise, a congregation can become a powerful witness even when it is in hiding. It only needs to remain consistent and perseverant. The virtue of this will shine through the persecution, deepening the discipleship of those in the congregation and touching those who see it. It will also give people in the congregation a stronger capacity to articulate their faith before others. This is because they will have experienced the presence and power of God in an immediate way.

Taking a page from its dealings with the financial crisis, First Church addressed their situation with the musician first by going to God in fasting and prayer. They laid out for God the dangers that surrounded them and asked God for help. They prayed especially that their witness for God's gracious work in Jesus Christ would not be harmed by whatever happened in relation to this situation, and they offered praise to God for not being subject to the whims and faults of humanity. They learned to recognize the power and presence of God in a new way, finding that no matter how difficult the situation became for them, God gave them the ability to endure it even if God did not take it away.

This was not a one-time prayer. The criminal case dragged on for months, along with the potential for a civil suit. During that time, as it became clear that the musician was guilty, the congregation members visited him in jail while also fully cooperating with the legal authorities to provide evidence and testimony. They never tried to shield him from his actions, but they did not abandon or vilify him, and they always had at least one representative who remained in the courtroom throughout the trial.

The congregation did retain a lawyer, and through the lawyer they reached out to the family of the abused child, offering to pay for counseling and any other needed care. These offers were met with silence. However, they never backed away from the offers.

In front of the media, they were gracious. They acknowledged the pain that had occurred in their building by one of their staff, and when they had slanderous charges brought against them they never responded in like manner. They simply sought to share the love of God as best they could and let the painful accusations fall away.

It took months, but in time, the judge sentenced the musician and he was taken to prison. The lawsuit threat was removed, and the media moved on to other things. However, First Church did not come out victorious in the sense that it had vanquished everyone who had attacked it or harmed it. Rather, it came out having overcome the danger by going into hiding, relying on God, and remaining missional by never letting its witness become soiled through partaking in the same violence that was marshaled against it.

Key Tactics: How to Engage in Missional Retreat

- Don't despair. Instead, use desperate circumstances as a motivator to rely on God.
- Don't rush to quick fixes. Take time to discern the larger vision of what God's purposes are and how your congregation can participate in them.

- Learn how to rely on God from Christians who have few resources (Christians from outside the United States, especially those under persecution, can be excellent teachers about this).
- Pray to God about your needs, asking for God's provision and protection.
- Fast to focus your prayer.
- Be patient for God's response.
- Be open to God, responding in many possible ways, including ways you might not expect.
- Remember, offering an alternative ethic by trusting in God *is* a witness to others of how powerful trusting in Jesus Christ is.
- Learn to praise God for the victory even in the midst of pain.

CHAPTER TWO

FOLLOW GOD'S LEAD

Exodus 4:27, 7:15
Joshua 6:22

On December 1, 2010, Rachel Maddow ran a segment on her MSNBC show called "Touched by a Televangelist." It included a Televangelist Infidelity Matrix that listed the names of four prominent televangelists and cross-referenced them with the forms of immorality they had confessed, including adultery, financial fraud, and drug use. The same year, news of child abuse by Catholic priests throughout Europe broke, adding to the outrage that had already been stoked by revelations of child abuse by priests in the United States. The issue grew so severe that Pope Benedict XVI issued a formal apology to those who were victims of abuse in Ireland as numerous priests were tried and convicted in civil courts in several European countries.

The reason that *evangelism* is an uncomfortable word for many of us today, even in the church, is partly because it has been associated with these scandals. None of us wants to be identified with people who were so clearly hypocrites. Their high-profile moral failures have already done enough damage to the way the Christian faith is viewed. It would be worse if we were seen as following in their footsteps by openly claiming the title of evangelist.

Scripture seems to side with us on this point. Ephesians 5:3 clearly states, "But fornication and impurity of any kind, or greed, must not even be mentioned among you, as is proper among saints." Based on this, it seems that God wants us to avoid being associated with people who have engaged in these sins. And, if those outside the church connect the dots between these sinners and the practice of evangelism, perhaps we should eschew evangelism as well.

I hope you can find the flaw in this logic.

The call of Ephesians is to avoid evil, not to avoid ministry! We are to avoid the practices—even the appearances—that cause people to question the goodness of the news we have to offer. However, we still need to offer that message.

It is true that evangelizing may cause us to be painted with the broad brush of an anti-evangelism feeling. However, that is far less likely than most of us think. Statistics show that 78 percent of unchurched people (those who have not attended church in the last six months other than for a special occasion or holiday) are open to having a conversation about faith with a friend.[1] The key issue here is that the conversation is with someone they trust who tries his or her best to live according to the faith. If we pattern our lives on our faith, avoiding the vices that plagued high-profile evangelists, people will not be so quick to lump our evangelism with theirs. They will see the authenticity of what we offer and respond accordingly.

Beyond earning the credibility to share our faith with our friends, maintaining our virtue as we evangelize is important because God's mission can lead us into unexpected places, including places often associated with sin. We go there because God wants the people in these places to become disciples of Jesus Christ too. But we will only be able to enter these places without people questioning our purity if we have lived virtuous lives.

Jesus gives us an excellent example of this in how he related to the Samaritan woman in John 4. A Jewish man, Jesus was associating with the wrong kind of person when he struck up a conversation with the Samaritan woman. The social awkwardness is seen

---

1   Bob Smietana, "Research: Unchurched Will Talk about Faith, Not Interested in Going to Church," LifeWay Research, June 28, 2016, http://lifewayresearch.com/2016/06/28 /unchurched-will-talk-about-faith-not-interested-in-going-to-church/.

in Jesus' disciples hesitation to broach the issue when they found him talking to her. According to the Gospel, "They were astonished that he was speaking with a woman, but no one said, 'What do you want?' or, 'Why are you speaking with her?'" (v. 27).

Even more remarkable than this initial meeting is what Jesus did next. After the woman testified about him to the rest of the villagers, and other Samaritans had come to talk to him, "they asked him to stay with them; and he stayed there two days" (v. 40). It was shocking enough that Jesus had spoken to a Samaritan woman. It would have been downright scandalous for him to stay in a Samaritan person's house, eat with Samaritans, and spend time with Samaritans. Yet that is what he did for two days.

I wonder what the disciples thought. They were, so far as we can tell, observant Jewish men of their age. They had no desire to impugn their own consciences or to disobey what they believed to be the laws God had established through Moses. Yet here they were challenged to stay with Jesus among the Samaritans if they were to be faithful to the mission of making disciples. It must have been a hard two days. Only the realization that they were honoring Jesus and that they had done their best to remain ritually pure throughout their lives would have helped ease their consciences as they dealt with this highly unexpected and uncomfortable turn of events.

We never get to read how the disciples spent those days. However, it is notable that no one seems to think less of Jesus or his disciples for their time with the Samaritans. Likely this was because Jesus and the disciples were well known for the purity they maintained in their lives. They were preserved from scandal because the one thing Jesus' opponents could not do is claim he was immoral. As for the disciples, for persevering with Jesus they were rewarded in the Samaritan village by seeing that "many more believed because of his [Jesus'] word" (v. 41).

The Great Commission requires that we remain pure. In that purity, it also calls us to go wherever people need to know what God has done in Jesus Christ and be invited to become disciples of Jesus. This could take us to the last place on earth that we expected to go.

First Church in the Hood

The leaders in First Church had decided to stay in prayer following the congregation's difficulties. The primary way they did this was to include prayer in their committee meetings. This was not just a prayer at the beginning of the meeting but an actual agenda item that set aside at least five minutes during the meetings to center on God and seek God's will for the congregation.

This practice of prayer had the unexpected result of bringing down the separation that had long existed between the programmatic and management committees. Rather than the worship, education, or outreach committees being seen as spiritual while the trustees, finance, and personnel committees were only seen as dealing with worldly issues, all the committees began to see themselves as engaged in God's mission as they sought to participate in God's purposes.

It was as this change was happening that the pastor returned from a conference and shared that First Church had been invited to be part of a joint vacation Bible school with a few other congregations. This seemed like an excellent opportunity for First Church, since its size made running a single-church VBS an exhausting process. However, there was a catch. The plan was to hold the VBS in a park that was in a crime-ridden part of town. In fact, there had been several muggings in the park and even a murder there the week prior. It was a place where few people from First Church ever ventured.

The idea of the joint VBS was to reach underserved children in that part of town. That seemed noble, but did the people of First Church really want to invite the children from their part of town to go somewhere that even the adults from First Church did not feel safe going?

Making the matter more complex was that all the people in First Church were white. The neighborhood surrounding the park was largely Hispanic. While a congregation located in that neighborhood would be involved in the VBS, the people of First Church wondered if the cultural divide meant they would have little to offer.

It was a difficult decision, and the committees agreed to spend two weeks in prayer before the pastor replied to the invitation. Several questions arose during this time. In addition to the danger of violent crime, what benefit would First Church receive? If there were new people who attended this VBS, wouldn't they be drawn to the congregation from that neighborhood? Given its own decline, First Church certainly could use new members! Could they afford to spend their resources on something that had virtually no chance of returning any increase to the congregation itself?

> The LORD said to Aaron, "Go into the wilderness to meet Moses." So he went; and he met him at the mountain of God and kissed him. Moses told Aaron all the words of the LORD with which he had sent him, and all the signs with which he had charged him. Then Moses and Aaron went and assembled all the elders of the Israelites. Aaron spoke all the words that the LORD had spoken to Moses, and performed the signs in the sight of the people. The people believed; and when they heard that the LORD had given heed to the Israelites and that he had seen their misery, they bowed down and worshiped. (Exod 4:27-31)

The people of First Church likely had a similar set of questions as Aaron had when he first heard God calling him to go into the wilderness and meet Moses. The call was for Aaron to go to the least hospitable place possible. It was bad enough for him to be a slave, but God called him to go meet his murderer brother in the middle of a desert. At least in Egypt there was food and water. He had to leave what little he had and travel to a land of deadly heat and lack of resources to meet a man who had committed a violent crime. Still, Aaron obeyed.

Once Aaron met Moses, things got worse. God called Aaron to return to the land of slavery and risk possible capture for having left to go into the wilderness! It would seem that God was calling Aaron to the worst possible situations.

We don't know how God spoke to Aaron or how quickly Aaron responded. All we know is that Aaron went. And here is the key thing: because he went, he heard "all the words of the LORD" and saw "all the signs" God had given Moses to perform. Aaron could not have heard God's words or seen God's power if he had not gone. He would have only heard the voice of God calling him to mission.

God never calls us to mission from behind but from in front of us. Remember, God is not only the Sending God but the sent God. God is already out and personally involved in the mission of redeeming creation, and God calls to us from the front lines of mission to join in that work. We never will see the power of God if we fail to heed God's voice calling us, because we will not be where God is doing the most remarkable things to accomplish God's purposes.

Beyond that, Aaron would not have had the opportunity to participate in God's bigger purposes if he had not obeyed God's initial command. All he knew at first was that he was called to meet Moses in the wilderness. His willingness to do this was the basis on which God made him a leader in the Exodus. By taking the first step of obedience toward mission, God introduced him to a far greater vision of what God was going to accomplish and gave him the gift of being at the center of that work.

Steps toward Solidarity

The people of First Church found themselves in a similar situation. After two weeks of prayer, and recalling the faithfulness of God to see them through the trials of the past few months, they decided they could not reject the invitation to participate in the VBS. They believed they heard the voice of God speak to them in this invitation, and they believed they would be disobedient to reject it.

Once they arrived at the park, they were grateful they had taken the time to discern God's voice calling them rather than just using a straightforward calculus of return on investment to decide whether they should participate in the VBS. There was a far greater need in the neighborhood than they anticipated. Not only were there a great many children who had not heard the message of the gospel or had Christians share God's love with them, daily life was also hard for all the people in the neighborhood.

Litter was strewn everywhere and the playground in the park was in disrepair. In addition to this, the children shared how they felt unsafe going to the park because it was often taken over by gangs in the evening. One little girl invited a congregation member from First Church to come and see the rest of the neighborhood. It was in little better shape than the park, including badly cracked sidewalks and streets. First Church members also had a chance to meet with the parents of the children. The parents spoke of the difficulties their children faced. The lack of public care for the park extended to the local schools, which were chronically short of supplies and had trouble attracting teachers. Places to shop for fresh produce were also lacking, making the neighborhood a food desert. The park was only four miles away from First Church, but it seemed like an entirely different world.

While the VBS did not have any grand miracle take place, the children and their parents both spoke of how wonderful it was to occupy the park for an entire week without fear. Occasionally they would point to clusters of people at the edge of the park and explain how they were made up of members of this or that gang but that the gangs had decided to leave the park alone during the week the churches were there. This was little short of a sign of God's presence in some people's minds.

The people of First Church saw just how open the people of this neighborhood were to receiving support and help. They didn't need outsiders to give them a better life, but they needed help creating an environment in which they could create a better life for themselves and their children. This led the people of First Church to consider what larger mission God might be calling them to undertake.

Drawn by the relationships that they were making, the volunteers from First Church decided to stay involved in the neighborhood surrounding the park following VBS. They started by learning more about the neighborhood, including how it had reached its present state.

They uncovered a sad history. Originally built as a neighborhood to house Eastern European immigrants coming to the area just before the First World War, the population had slowly changed as the more rural area around the town had attracted larger numbers of Hispanic migrant workers. These workers began to move into houses in the area, slowly replacing the heirs of the Eastern Europeans, who were moving to the city fifty miles away.

About two decades ago, after the neighborhood was almost entirely Hispanic, the town had decided to build a new bypass road that would make access to the closest interstate easier. Officials hoped this would attract new residents and money to the town. The most direct line for the new roadway cut through the town in a way that segmented off the neighborhood from the rest of the town. While some resistance was put up against this, the road was built as proposed. Some of the people in First Church even remembered being in favor of the decision because of the new wealth they thought it would attract.

The resulting segmentation made it harder for the people in the neighborhood to access the rest of the town, separating it from many of the town's amenities and stores. The property values in the neighborhood plummeted, and with less of a tax base and a more segregated population, the town began to pay less attention to the neighborhood. The result was what First Church encountered in the park.

The people of First Church began to discuss what they could do. They thought about adopting a school in the neighborhood, providing backpacks filled with supplies to neighborhood students, or partnering with the town food pantry to help provide more fresh food. However, as they discussed these ideas, it became clear that if First Church wanted to see a lasting change, they needed to move beyond caring for immediate needs. They needed to address the deeper structural issues that had taken the capacity for choice and advancement away from the people in the neighborhood. This would mean getting involved in the local political scene.

Initially, the pastor and leadership at First Church resisted this idea. They pointed out that the church was to be a spiritual entity, not a political one. Wouldn't becoming political violate the tax-exempt status they had? They were also worried that it would cause fault lines within the congregation as political leanings, usually kept quiet, were aired. In addition, it might hurt their chance to grow because people in their neighborhood would view them as some sort of activist organization.

However, they kept coming back to the call of Jesus to love their neighbors. The people in the segmented neighborhood were their neighbors. They had not realized this prior to the VBS, but they did now. And, if they were to love their neighbors, they felt they also had to take seriously the command in James 2:15-17: "If a brother or sister is naked and lacks daily food, and one of you says to them, "Go in peace; keep warm and eat your fill," and yet you do not supply their bodily needs, what is the good of that?" Here were brothers and sisters who needed not just food and clothes, but education and opportunity. The only way to obey this missional mandate was through engaging in the political process.

> Then the LORD said to Moses, "Pharaoh's heart is hardened; he refuses to let the people go. Go to Pharaoh in the morning, as he is going out to the water; stand by at the river bank to meet him, and take in your hand the staff that was turned into a snake. Say to him, 'The LORD, the God of the Hebrews, sent me to you to say, "Let my people go, so that they may worship me in the wilderness." But until now you have not listened. Thus says the LORD, "By this you shall know that I am the LORD." See, with the staff that is in my hand I will strike the water that is in the Nile, and it shall be turned to blood. The fish in the river shall die, the river itself shall stink, and the Egyptians shall be unable to drink water from the Nile.'" (Exod 7:14-18)

Aaron found himself in a similar place alongside Moses. Having inspired hope in the people when they came with God's message, their next step was to go to another place they had never expected: to Pharaoh. Only Pharaoh had the human authority to free the Israelites from their slavery in Egypt.

Entering the presence of Pharaoh, especially as a slave with an unpopular message, was no easy task. There was no leverage that Aaron or Moses had to induce Pharaoh to accept their demands. All they had was their trust that God was stronger than Pharaoh.

Approaching Pharaoh this way also left Moses and Aaron no way out personally. They had to identify completely with the people of Israel and their demands on Israel's behalf. Whatever happened to the people would happen to them. Otherwise their mission would be ineffective. If they were not fully invested in the outcome and had left a way open so they could escape if things went poorly with Pharaoh, neither the Israelites nor the Egyptians would have taken them seriously. As it was, they stood in solidarity with people who had fewer options than they did for how to live.

Moses and Aaron also got to know Pharaoh. While the relationship might have been tenuous and combative, they nonetheless developed a relationship. From this, they had a sense for how to position themselves based on Pharaoh's demeanor. The first time they had an audience with him, they laid out their basic demands and demonstrated the power of God to support that position. When that did not work, as we see in this passage, they listened to God and upped the ante. They brought a stronger demonstration of power to show that Pharaoh's refusal not only hurt the people of Israel but all of Egypt. When the Nile turned to blood, no one could drink from it and even the fish in it died. They made it clear that Pharaoh's decision was not just about granting freedom to a suffering people but about protecting his own people.

The rest of the story is well known. Pharaoh's heart continued to be hard, and the result was nine more plagues that swept through Egypt. During this time Pharaoh continued to negotiate with Moses and Aaron, seeking to bargain them down on their demands: first just to let the people go and offer sacrifices to the LORD and then return (Exod 8:8, 28), then for only the men to leave (10:11), and then for all the people to go without their livestock (10:24). Moses and Aaron refused these offers, insisting that only the fullness of God's purpose was acceptable. Anything less would be an affront to God and God's people. This leads to the heavy blow of the curse on the firstborn and the Exodus.

If part of our commission to make disciples includes our congregation standing with those who have fewer resources, we can learn from how Aaron and Moses carried out their commission from God. They did it primarily by building relationships, both with the powerful and with those in need.

First, we can build relationships with those who are in power. This need not be adversarial, as it was with Aaron, Moses, and Pharaoh. In the United States, political leaders often welcome people connecting with them through attending public meetings or writing letters. The credibility these relationships generate for us with public officials is essential. If a day comes when we must stand before those leaders to advocate for a change, it allows everyone in the room to know each other and have a sense of what to expect from each other. This opens the way for conversation.

Being in a relationship with those who have power should not lull us into thinking that our privileged place is more important to God's work than our advocacy on behalf of those in need. Just as Moses and Aaron identified with the Israelites on whose behalf they spoke, so we need to stand firmly together with those for whom we advocate. This leads us to the second relationship we need to build: one of solidarity with the needy.

When we stand in solidarity with the needy, we refuse to exercise our ability to drop out of our advocacy when times become uncomfortable. We also refuse to accept anything less from those in power than everything that the needy require.

One reason for refusing to back down from our demands is because our missional work on behalf of others is part of our mission to share God's love with everyone. In working to release the oppression of a few, we are working for the benefit of all. Both the oppressed and the oppressors are set free from the structures that force them into their respective roles. Both are also set free to recognize the gracious power of God and to become disciples of Jesus Christ.

The Children's Defense Fund's *Ending Child Poverty Now* (2016) document offers an excellent example of how a secular advocacy group frames its advocacy on behalf of poor children in terms of helping all Americans. As chapter 1 explains,

> Reducing child poverty would yield incalculable benefits
> for millions of children and the country as a whole . . .

eliminating child poverty between the prenatal years and age 5 would increase lifetime earnings between $53,000 and $100,000 per child, for a total lifetime benefit of $20 to $36 billion for all babies born in a given year. And we can never measure the countless innovations and discoveries that did not occur because children's potentials were stunted by poverty.[2]

Advocacy that seeks for others to be treated with basic human dignity and given equal opportunities to advance in life always has benefits for those beyond the specific people being advocated for. We advocate for the benefit of all when we advocate for the benefit of a specific group.

As we do this, we must avoid the temptation of believing that we are operating in our own power. The political and economic structures of the world are seductive; they convince us that we can shape our own lives and the lives of others.

Moses and Aaron were constantly reminded that God was the primary force freeing Israel by the miraculous plagues that burst upon Egypt. While we may not have such grand supernatural displays during our advocacy, we can follow Moses' example of remaining in prayer throughout our missional work. This helps us avoid losing sight of the presence and power of God as we navigate the political realm.

First Church sought to do this. A group of its members began to attend town council meetings and school board meetings, getting to know the various officials. As they met, they began to lend their voices to amplify the concerns of the people in the segmented neighborhood. At first they were dismissed with a nod and a smile. The idea of doing good for the neighborhood was nice, but it was not realistic. After all, there were bills to be paid and schools in other neighborhoods were doing quite well. Why take away resources from successful schools and neighborhoods to care for a place that was failing?

---

2   Children's Defense Fund, "Ending Child Poverty Now," http://www.childrensdefense.org /library/PovertyReport/EndingChildPovertyNow.html#sthash.5CNHdpy2.dpuf, 2016.

The volunteers from First Church were not to be dissuaded. Remaining in prayer while fostering their relationships with those in the neighborhood and with local political leaders, they developed workable plans that would provide better nutrition and schools for the children in the neighborhood. It did not happen quickly, but steady progress began to take shape. As this occurred, the community leaders from the neighborhood began to take new heart and join back in the work of advocating for their own children. Other organizations also took note, and there was an effort toward developing a collective impact strategy that would allow them to work from their various areas of expertise to accomplish a few specific and measurable goals around literacy and nutrition. As the influence of these groups became more significant, the school board and town council began to come around in their positions.

First Church did not end up being the primary organization in helping this neighborhood, nor did its advocacy work stay at the forefront. While First Church volunteers remained active, they gave way to the neighborhood's local leadership and to other organizations that were better equipped for this work. Still, their persistence in prayer and advocacy paid off, helping to provide a voice for people who were next door, but who had long been forgotten.

Dealing with the Wrong People

One of the most common complaints about Jesus was that he spent time with sinners. Religious leaders frequently pointed this out, arguing that if he were a prophet, he would know just how bad these people were and would avoid them, especially given how moral Jesus was in his own life. Unpersuaded by this logic, Jesus provided a response so succinct and potent that three of the Gospel writers recorded it: "Those who are well have no need of a physician, but those who are sick. . . . I have come to call not the righteous but sinners" (Matt 9:12-13; also, Mark 2:17; Luke 5:31-32).

The point Jesus made was that God's purpose entailed inviting all people into the kingdom, regardless of how sinful they might be. Those who sinned were to repent and be forgiven. Those who did not need this forgiveness would be able to enter on their own.

Of course, the religious leaders missed the irony of this statement. The fact that Jesus ate with them as well as with the sinners suggests that Jesus saw all of them as sick and in need of becoming his disciples!

Jesus saw little difference in preaching to the Pharisees or the prostitutes. All of them needed forgiveness. He went to everyone, regardless of who they were, to carry out God's mission of making disciples.

This was a hard lesson for First Church. During the time First Church was working with the segmented neighborhood, the church leaders had become stricter about how the church was perceived in public. This was because of the lingering negative ideas about the church from the child abuse scandal and because the church had begun to engage in more visible political work in the town. As one of the matrons of the church put it, "If I needed to go to the bathroom badly, I would sooner find a bush than go into one of the bars in town. What would people think if they saw me coming out of a bar?" While not quite to this extreme, several of the people in the congregation were of a similar opinion.

At the same time, First Church was beginning to garner the attention of younger people in the town because of its work in the neighborhood. They were impressed that this little congregation seemed to be looking beyond itself and working to make the world a better place without proselytizing. After a few months of watching, a dozen of the young adults invited one of the church leaders who had been especially prominent in advocating for the neighborhood to join them for drinks at the local pub. They also invited the pastor.

The pastor and the member were uncertain what to do. Initially, the pastor politely invited the young adults to gather at the church building instead, offering them a home-cooked dinner if they came. The young adults responded that they met frequently at the pub, and it would avoid confusion if they could just meet in their regular place. They knew everyone would be there. The pastor gently intimated that he and the member did not drink alcohol. The young adults didn't mind that in the least. They would enjoy their own drinks but did not expect the pastor or church member to drink.

Unsure of what else to do, the pastor and church member decided to go. They thought it was better for two of them to be there so that they could vouch for each other in case the media caught wind of just one of them going and reported it. The pastor also decided to wear a clerical collar for added moral authority.

There is no question that the be-collared clergyman raised a few eyebrows as he made his way into the pub along with his parishioner. The pastor began wondering if wearing the collar was such a good idea. If he had gone in a regular shirt and tie he would have drawn less attention.

The young adults were pleased to see the First Church representatives and waved them over to their table. It was clear that the young adults had already had a round of drinks, and they ordered a fresh set when their guests arrived. They invited the pastor and member to get anything they wanted. They each settled for an iced tea and, when the drinks arrived, the conversation began. As it did, the pastor wondered nervously if God was pleased he was in a pub.

> Joshua said to the two men who had spied out the land, "Go into the prostitute's house, and bring the woman out of it and all who belong to her, as you swore to her." So the young men who had been spies went in and brought Rahab out, along with her father, her mother, her brothers, and all who belonged to her—they brought all her kindred out— and set them outside the camp of Israel. (Josh 6:22-23)

The spies from Joshua had a hard job. They had to enter enemy territory in Jericho and come back with intelligence that Joshua and the Israelite military could use. While there they found themselves cornered, being tracked by the authorities of Jericho. Their only hope was to accept the invitation to hide in a prostitute's house. Rahab, the prostitute, was true to her word and kept them safe when the authorities came knocking. She told the spies she did this because she had heard of the power of their God and would rather join them than to trust the city walls to keep the army of Israel at bay.

For her kindness and courage on their behalf, the spies gave Rahab a scarlet rope and told her to hang it outside her window on the day of the attack. She and anyone else in her house would be spared.

When the walls of Jericho collapsed, God left Rahab's house intact, and the army of Israel was faithful not to harm Rahab and her family. When the battle was over, Joshua commanded the spies to bring out Rahab and her family in safety.

In the context of the story, Joshua's command makes sense. However, without that context it is strange indeed: go visit a prostitute in her house! Would God really call people to do that? The answer is yes. God called them to do this because the people in that house were a part of God's mission to redeem all people. God wanted Rahab and her family to know and proclaim the faithfulness of God just as much as God wanted the heirs of Abraham to know and proclaim it. To do that, God unflinchingly sent God's people to a prostitute's house as part of God's mission.

Not only were Rahab and her family saved, but God welcomed them to be fruitful parts of God's mission. The Gospel of Matthew records that Rahab would marry an Israelite man named Salmon, and they would become direct ancestors of Jesus Christ. God's people do not just go into unlikely places to redeem the people there, but to invite those people to become disciples who will be part of the redemptive work of God in the world.

The pastor from First Church soon learned this lesson. As the pastor was describing the involvement of the church in the neighborhood, two local men came over to the table. Taking a good look at the pastor, they began to ridicule him openly for his church's involvement with the child abuse case. One of them had heard how the congregation members had continued to visit the musician in prison even after he was convicted. He was disgusted that a congregation would support a child molester like that and asked what kind of God the congregation believed in.

The pastor was already ill at ease in the pub and was entirely taken off guard by this onslaught. He stumbled over a few words but was at a loss to respond. As his face began to turn bright red, he was shocked to hear several of the young adults come to his defense. They argued that whatever had happened at the church with the musician, the fact that this congregation loved children was plain enough from the efforts they had made in the segmented neighborhood. They said that the sort of consistent work they did there was louder evidence to the kind of God the congregation worshiped than any one-time scandal that had happened in the church building or because of a church employee.

Confronted by these unexpected defenders, the two angry men hurled a few more insults and departed. The young adults apologized to the pastor and the member. They then said that they had been discussing how they might be able to help in the neighborhood work. This confrontation had convinced them that they needed to act on that. They asked the pastor what next steps they could take. As the pastor spoke with them about this, he realized that without anyone from the church sharing the gospel with them directly, First Church had prompted these young people to become disciples through their advocacy work.

Key Tactics: How to Follow God's Lead

- Remain in prayer. It is always God's power that accomplishes the mission work a congregation does.
- Obey the simplest promptings to be in mission.
- Be open to going places in mission that make you uncomfortable.
- Build relationships with the people with whom you are in mission.
- Look for needs you can meet immediately.
- Do some problem solving: figure out why people have the immediate needs that they do.
- Be open to engaging in ways to change the systematic problems people face, including getting involved in political and economic processes. Mostly this means being committed to attending meetings and voicing what you think is best.
- Stand in solidarity with those who are in need. This means staying related to them over the long haul, making their concerns your own. Be there to suffer with them when they are hurting and celebrate with them when all goes well.

- Build relationships with the people who are in power, especially if you come from a social or cultural position that has easy access to those people. These relationships will make formal meetings and requests go much more smoothly.
- Demonstrate the ways that granting justice to one group is in the best interest of all people. You are not pleading for one special group on God's behalf. You are working for the redemption of all people in God's mission.
- Do not bargain away God's purpose. Once you have prayed and received an assurance of what God's vision is for the situation, stick to it. Remember that God is in the mission too, and God will bring about what God desires. We need to persevere until God accomplishes this.
- Be open to meet with everyone. We are called to make disciples of all people, and we cannot do this if we rule out engaging with people, especially if they are interested in the work of God.
- Be prepared for resistance.

GET CONSECRATED

Leviticus 10:9
Joshua 4:5

The book of Revelation reads like the script for a musical. After an opening prologue of John writing letters to the churches, the curtain is drawn to reveal an action-packed series of events punctuated by the inhabitants of heaven breaking into song. Chapters 4-5, 7, 11-12, 15-16, and 19 all describe this heavenly worship. The celestial beings offer thanks for the good that God is doing and acknowledge the majesty of God's character.

In between these times of worship, the angels, saints, and others are working alongside God to wipe away all remnants of evil and to establish God's kingdom in its fullness. In other words, they are participating in God's mission. This shows us that worship and mission go hand-in-hand, each supporting the other. Worship is essential if we are to be missional.

I confess that I have not always seen worship as so important. I thought worship was boring when I was a kid (and as an adult I don't always have a better opinion of it!). This is because worship is so often disconnected from mission. Aside from a possible announcement about mission activities the congregation supports, worship is often treated as the opposite of going into mission. It is more a consumer activity, as seen in the term *worship service*. A service is something someone else does for you, like a full-service gas station where the attendants pump your gas and clean your windows. Likewise, many of us experience worship as a service performed by professionals who pray, read the Bible, and sing praises for us. We do not know it as an initiation into the presence of God and God's mission.

Congregations that fret over whether their worship service is seeker-friendly or contemporary enough miss the point. If worship is no more than a service, and if a service is just something professionals provide for people, then people will find worship lacking regardless of its style. This may not happen right away if a congregation has high production values for their worship services, but if the primary work people are asked to do in worship is simply to consume the service, a congregation will need to make their services bigger, better, and more exciting to keep people coming. This is the opposite of the call of God for congregations to be missional. Consumer logic and missional logic do not mix.

The primary reason that worship becomes unhinged from mission is because congregations forget that God is present when God's people worship. Jesus made it clear that God shows up every time disciples are together: "For where two or three are gathered in my name, I am there among them" (Matt 18:20). This includes worship. When we ignore God's active presence, worship becomes just a repetition of rituals and words that have little connection to the outside world. This makes it easy to segment worship away as a chore we do once a week rather than to see it as something that influences how we live.

If God is with us as we worship, that should change everything. Our worship opens the door for us to enter God's holiness as a congregation. We praise God together for that holiness, and we allow God to consecrate us to be carriers of that holiness as we serve in God's mission of making disciples. Consecration is the act of setting something aside for holy use. The tabernacle and the various altar implements used for worship by the Israelites were consecrated in a special ceremony. Likewise, Aaron and the priests were consecrated for their ordained ministry (Lev 8).

Like the Israelite priests, Jesus consecrates us for the holy work of mission when we gather in his presence. We see a picture of this in the Gospel of John, which tells us that Jesus "breathed on them [the disciples] and said to them, 'Receive the Holy Spirit'" (20:22). More than just teaching and empowering his disciples, Jesus consecrated them with the Holy Spirit, setting them apart for the holy work of making disciples and transforming them internally, so their lives were consistent with their mission.

We still have special acts of worship to consecrate people for the holy work of mission. Baptism, commissioning, and ordination are unique moments when we as a people of God acknowledge and celebrate God's consecrating power for specific individuals. However, consecration is not just reserved for select individuals or for specific acts of worship. All of us can seek and celebrate God's consecration during our regular times of worship. This is important because consecration is not a one-time event. We sometimes need to be re-consecrated. God understands this. There are even rules in the Old Testament for how the priests could renew their consecration if they became ritually impure (for example, Num 6).

Remember, the Great Commission in Matthew tells us to serve as witnesses "as we are going" throughout our daily lives. The missional tactic of being consecrated regularly through worship is important for us to avoid losing our focus on carrying God's holy gift of discipleship to others. Every time we gather to worship we should come prepared to be consecrated for our ongoing participation in God's mission.

This work of consecration suggests that many of our congregations need to shift their thinking about worship. Historically, worship has been the "front door" of the church, serving as the primary act people were invited to attend. For this reason, worship attendance has been our primary statistic for determining how healthy a congregation is.

While there is a public aspect to worship, worship is less about connecting with those outside the church than about being in the presence of God. I realize this is a controversial statement. There are some congregations that use their Sunday worship as their primary means to connect with new people. This is fine, provided these congregations also provide worship geared toward bringing those who are already disciples into the consecrating presence of God. It does not matter when we create time for our own entrance into consecration through worship, it just matters that we do it.

If we cannot run multiple times of worship, my point is not to say that our congregations should be sloppy or unmindful of how we welcome visitors into our worship, but that we should be primarily concerned with whether we are seeking God as we worship. Relating authentically to the presence of God will be the most powerful witness to those who may be visitors to our congregations. Rather than hoping to impress visitors with our music or preaching, we can welcome the visitors to be in awe of the God we worship.

According to Jesus, we fail to be missional if we do *not* focus on being consecrated for God's work. As he put it, "Those who abide in me and I in them bear much fruit" (John 15:5). Unless we spend time abiding in Jesus, being consecrated to his holy work, we will not be effective in his mission. Worship is the primary way we can do this.

Even though Jesus was holy, he modeled the importance of being consecrated through worship. We see this when he went to John for baptism. While John made it clear that Jesus did not need to be baptized, Jesus explained his baptism was an opportunity for him to "fulfill all righteousness" (Matt 3:15). This suggests that Jesus was baptized at least partly as an act of consecration. God desired to acknowledge him publicly and to set him aside for a dedicated time of mission.

Following his baptism, Jesus continued to seek God's consecration. While he was in the wilderness, even though there was no one to worship alongside him, Jesus turned to God by meditating on the Scriptures. It was by receiving God's consecration through the Scriptures that Jesus was prepared to face Satan, as seen by his use of scriptural quotations to respond to Satan's temptations.

Both at the start of his ministry and throughout it, Jesus intentionally dedicated time to seek God's consecration so he could be useful in God's mission. This consecration was not just preparatory to the mission; it was part of the mission. By setting this example, Jesus made it clear that his followers would not be equipped to call people to be his disciples if they did not consistently seek consecration.

The need for his disciples to be consecrated became even clearer when Jesus commanded his earliest followers to stay in Jerusalem until they were "clothed with power from on high" (Luke 24:49). These earliest disciples needed to receive a consecrating "baptism of fire" through the coming of the Holy Spirit at Pentecost. In preparation for receiving this, they gathered daily in prayer and worship. Even after the coming of the Spirit, they continued to gather regularly for worship, availing themselves of God's consecrating power as they shared at table fellowship and attended to the teaching of the apostles (Acts 2:43-47, 4:33). Congregations today can continue this practice of seeking God's consecration through worship so they will be able to carry out God's holy mission.

Seeking Worship Leaders

Following the pastor's experience in the pub, several of the young adults began joining the members from First Church who were involved with the Hispanic neighborhood. Over the course of a few weeks, the relationships between the young adults and the people from First Church led to the young adults becoming interested in attending worship one Sunday morning. The members were thrilled to hear this and encouraged them to come, even offering to buy them lunch afterward. When the excited members told the pastor about this, he was pleased. However, he also began to think about his experience in the pub. Clearly, the young adults were not used to attending worship in a church. He wondered what sort of impression worship at First Church would make on them. The worship was not bad but was typical Protestant fare that assumed people knew how to use the hymnal (and knew the hymns in it) and were familiar with the order of worship. He wondered if it would make sense to those outside First Church's usual members.

The pastor did a quick hunt on the Internet and skimmed some old books from an evangelism course he had taken in seminary. He found lots of references to making worship more accessible to visitors, such as by printing the words of prayers in the bulletin, having good signage around the church, and having greeters who would connect with people as soon as they exited their cars in the parking lot. These all seemed like good ideas to the pastor, but they also seemed simple. He wondered if there wasn't something more.

He spoke with some members of the church, who agreed to visit the bigger churches in town to see what they were doing to connect with visitors. The following week, when the members returned, they brought stories of services that were "seeker-sensitive." This meant that they not only had good signage and greeters, but that everything in the worship service was focused on people who were not used to being in a church building or at a church activity. This included removing symbols (such as crosses), unfamiliar vocabulary, and undue pressure to convert to a specific way of living. In addition, the congregations sought to impress the new people with the quality of music and other elements of the service. These tactics seemed to work. All the churches were relatively full, and some were growing.

As the group discussed these possibilities, they began to feel uneasy. They could understand wanting worship to be excellent. Why should people expect second-class music or public speaking just because they were in the church? At the same time they wondered whether this sort of worship tactic got to the heart of the pastor's concerns. They could see how it would be helpful to people who wanted a zero-depth entry point when visiting a congregation, but was it the best way to live into their mission? After all, worship was not just for first-time visitors but for the people who had attended church for decades and sought to be consecrated as disciples. Was there another way?

> And the LORD spoke to Aaron: Drink no wine or strong drink, neither you nor your sons, when you enter the tent of meeting, that you may not die; it is a statute forever throughout your generations. You are to distinguish between the holy and the common, and between the unclean and the clean; and you are to teach the people of Israel all the statutes that the LORD has spoken to them through Moses. (Lev 10:8-11)

The first five books of the Bible are full of laws that dictate how people are to live. These include laws that seem downright odd today, such as those that define what makes people ceremonially clean (rinsing with water and waiting outside the camp for a certain number of days) or unclean (touching a dead body, eating certain foods, and so on).

God gave these laws to the people in order for them to consecrate their daily lives by their obedience. God, represented by the tabernacle at the center of the camp, was traveling with them through the wilderness. The presence of God made the people holy, and they needed to order their lives in a way that reflected that holiness.

The laws were even stricter for the priests. Aaron and his sons did not just travel alongside the tabernacle but entered it on behalf of the people. This included Aaron entering the Holy of Holies once a year. To carry out this work the priests needed to live even more carefully.

This passage from Leviticus explains that the priests had an additional reason for their unique laws. It was not just that they were going to be in the presence of God, but that they were going to be God's representatives among the people. They were on a mission to teach God's people about what was holy and what was not, guiding the people of Israel from being unclean to clean, from being sinful to holy. Part of that mission was to manifest holiness in their own lives. This was not just a preparation for mission; it was part of their mission. Without this ongoing consecration, they would not be effective witnesses of the difference God made in the life of Israel.

For congregations today, this means that before we talk about worship, we need to start by talking about the leaders of the church. Church leaders who seek God's consecration on a regular basis to live holy lives are essential for a congregation to become missional. This is because a congregation that wants to be effective in God's mission to make disciples of Jesus Christ must first be full of people who are already disciples of Jesus Christ. The leaders set the standard of holy living for the people in the congregation, and the congregation sets the standard of holy living for the people they invite into discipleship.

Leaders who are more visible, such as pastors and worship leaders, must be especially committed to living a holy life. They must model the desire to praise God and seek God's consecration even as they lead worship. They should be excellent in their duties, whether as musicians, liturgists, or preachers, but that excellence should be in service of seeking God's consecration so they can be useful in God's mission. It should never be for personal fame.

Personnel committees should be intentional about vetting not only the competencies of worship leaders but their desire to grow in holiness. Do they understand God is present with them? Do they see themselves as participating in the mission of God by leading worship? Do their lives show evidence of seeking to live according to God's will? Once leaders are hired, they should be given opportunities to seek God's consecration as part of their professional development. This will all have an impact on how they lead worship and how capable the congregation is to participate in God's mission.

Along with selecting and encouraging these sorts of leaders, a congregation should redefine how it measures whether worship has been successful. For Aaron and his sons, there would have been all sorts of ways to define success. Did the bread of the presence come out of the oven looking good? Did the incense smell just right? Was the number of people coming to sacrifice thank offerings to God increasing?

However, instead of looking at these exterior issues, the verses from Leviticus make it clear that the only item that mattered was whether the people knew God's laws and were striving to obey them by living holy lives. To put this another way, the success of worship was measured in the holiness of people's everyday lives.

Today, we are often asked to count the numbers in attendance, the amount gathered in the offering, and other items related to worship. Consequently, our inclination is to build bigger, louder, more elaborate and entertaining worship services to drive up those numbers. There is a serious problem with this. Not only does this thinking reinforce the idea of worship as a "service," it almost entirely delinks worship from being part of a larger mission. Certainly, we want to worship with energy and excellence, but the success of worship is not found in counting the things of worship. It is found in whether the worship facilitates people coming into the presence of God for praise and consecration. If it does, then it allows them to extend their witness for Jesus Christ by calling people to become his disciples.

We can ask several questions to test if our worship is part of our mission. Do we share with each other about the goodness of God through Jesus Christ (whether by song, prayer, liturgy, testimony, and so on)? Do those who visit have a time to interact with us and hear the good news shared again after worship? Do we understand that when we share in the means of grace, especially Communion, we are receiving God's consecration for missionary work? Do we have rituals to acknowledge those who have reached milestones in their faith and to commission those being sent out to share the gospel in specific ways?

First Church decided to ask questions such as these. Rather than become seeker-sensitive by minimizing their message to make it easier for new people to accept, the pastor gathered the worship leaders so they could distill the essence of who they were as Christians and what they believed God called them to be and do. Based on this they sought to infuse each act of worship with intentionality around participating in the mission of God. They made certain their songs praised God rather than focused on human agency. In their prayers they thanked God for where they already saw God at work and petitioned God to complete God's purposes. They welcomed a variety of people to speak, sharing what God was doing in their lives. They used their offering time to share about how they had seen God work through the congregation. In all these things, they sought first to praise God, and second, to help those in attendance recognize that they were consecrated as individuals and as a congregation. This made worship a way to invigorate people in mission.

They also decided to make use of their Christian vocabulary and symbols. They recognized that this would not be an authentic expression of faith for some congregations. However, they felt they could better seek God's consecration with the aid of traditional vocabulary and symbols that helped them focus on the presence of

God. To bridge the gap that visitors might feel when encountering these uniquely Christian words and symbols, the congregation did its best to interpret their meanings through pamphlets in the pews and notes in the bulletins, as well as through people who volunteered to sit next to visitors to help guide them through the liturgy.

Seeking Worship, Prompting Evangelism

First Church's effort at linking worship with mission had two interesting results. First, it dramatically increased the capacity of the people already in the congregation to express their faith. As they sharpened the focus of their songs, preaching, and prayers, and more people in the congregation shared testimonies of how they were relating to God, they became more comfortable with the concepts and vocabulary of the Christian faith.

Second, it had a curious effect on the young adult visitors. They found the worship inspiring, but they also felt it was something alien to them. This was not because they couldn't understand the language, symbols, or practices the congregation used, since the members of First Church explained what they did and why they did it. Rather, the setting for worship in a church building and the traditional music and liturgy did not feel natural to them.

Based on this, the young adults approached the pastor and asked about an alternative. At first the pastor thought they wanted a second worship time, but the young adults had something more radical in mind. They said that the pub was where they felt most comfortable. It was their "third place," somewhere that was neither home nor work, but that allowed for good relationships and conversations. Would First Church support them in establishing an authentic and inspiring worship time at the pub?

After his initial experience visiting with the young adults, the pastor had mostly gotten over his discomfort with the pub. He and some of the other members had even visited with the young adults there a couple more times. However, could someone worship there? Would God be honored in a place like that? Could Christians be consecrated for mission if they were surrounded by drinking, even drunkenness and other vices? Plus, even if worship could happen there, the worshipers would be surrounded by a situation that was outside of their control and could easily distract them.

> Then Joshua summoned the twelve men from the Israelites, whom he had appointed, one from each tribe. Joshua said to them, "Pass on before the ark of the LORD your God into the middle of the Jordan, and each of you take up a stone on his shoulder, one for each of the tribes of the Israelites, so that this may be a sign among you. When your children ask in time to come, 'What do those stones mean to you?' then you shall tell them that the waters of the Jordan were cut off in front of the ark of the covenant of the LORD. When it crossed over the Jordan, the waters of the Jordan were cut off. So these stones shall be to the Israelites a memorial forever." (Josh 4:4-7)

When the people of Israel prepared to enter the Promised Land, they needed to cross the Jordan River at flood stage. As they camped along the banks, God told Joshua that, as with Moses and the Red Sea, God would lead the people through the Jordan on dry land. Unlike with Moses, God would not have Joshua hold out a staff to part the waters. Rather, the priests had to enter the river bearing the Ark of the Covenant with them. Only once their feet entered the water would the river be stopped.

With Moses, the people could see the dry land before they started walking. With Joshua, at least the first group of people had to get wet before the dry land appeared. God called them to trust that God would appear in power; however, they only would see that power after they had committed themselves to obeying God.

This is a powerful lesson for going into mission. There are times when the work we are called to seems like foolhardiness. It will tax our resources and expose us to uncertain, uncomfortable, and unpredictable situations. God promises to be with us, but we will not see God or God's power until we have stepped into a place beyond our control.

We encounter this sort of promise and call to trust in large and small ways. One of the smaller ways (though it can seem large as we do it) can be changing how we worship.

We often want to script worship carefully. Our reasons for this are usually well intentioned: if worship is about approaching the presence of God, then we want to give God our best. We should be thoughtful and careful with our words and deeds so we can best honor God. In addition to this, the way we worship often becomes comfortable for a congregation. To change it is not only potentially to give less than our best to God, it is to disrupt the patterns and relationships that the people in the congregation have.

It is good for us to desire excellence and congregational engagement in worship, but we must always remember that our ways of worshiping are a means to enter the presence of God, not the end. If we become too concerned with how we worship, we turn worship into an idol. We can even become idolatrous about worship by insisting on worship practices we think are necessary to call people to discipleship, like having only certain styles of music or preaching.

If God wants us to worship differently than we planned or than we are used to, we need to obey. It may be uncomfortable for us when we make the change, but the promise for Joshua and Israel is the same promise for us: God will make a way for us to move forward if we obey. This is especially important because worship is not only about being in the presence of God but also a way of participating in God's mission. To resist God's call for new ways of worshiping is also to sabotage our ability to receive God's consecration.

While it is a different activity than worshiping, the same point relates to evangelism. Going out to evangelize can be a companion activity to worship. In worship, we enter the presence of God through corporate acts of spiritual formation (praying, singing, meditating on the Scriptures, speaking the truth to one another, receiving the sacraments, and so on) to praise God and be consecrated by God. In evangelism, we enter the presence of God by going into the world where Jesus commissioned us to be witnesses, and we rely explicitly on God to consecrate others as they become disciples. Both the evangelistic mission field and the worship space are holy ground. Both are places we can meet and experience the presence of God. Both are places where we first must step out in trust to see God's power revealed.

Given how uncomfortable many of us are sharing the gospel with others, this promise that God will meet us as we move in trust should be especially helpful. Instead of waiting for God to do something miraculous to prompt us to evangelize, we should expect the miraculous to happen *after* we have taken the first step to obey God's call to proclaim the gospel.

The Bible is full of examples of those who saw God's power after obeying. Abram set out from his father's house to an unknown land based on God's promise to bless him once he got there (Gen 12:1-3) and years later received the son he and Sarai had always wanted. Gideon was told to fight against the more powerful Midianite army with only the promise that God would be with him (Judg 6:16), and he emerged with a great victory because of God's intervention. David went to face Goliath armed with the assurance that God was mightier than the giant (1 Sam 17:45-47), and he became a powerful witness to both the Israelites and the Philistines as to God's power when he prevailed. The entire people of Israel were promised that if they returned from exile to Jerusalem, God would protect them (Isa 43:2), so they could rebuild the Temple as a witness to the nations.

To do evangelism we need to trust that the Holy Spirit is with us. It is the Spirit who will convict, convince, and teach those we evangelize to live holy lives as disciples of Jesus Christ. Often, this means that once we have shared, we need to stand back. We should remain available to encourage and guide, but we should do this only when needed. Otherwise, we trust God will bear fruit in the most appropriate way, creating a community of disciples who obey the teachings of Jesus faithfully within its context.

This new community may look different from our congregations. That is OK! Our congregations today don't look anything like the congregations of the early church. They do not even look like each other (think of the difference in worship among Eastern Orthodox, Roman Catholic, and Pentecostal congregations). We all worship by our own patterns and express our faith in our own ways. Yet we all serve the same Triune God through Jesus Christ in the power of the Holy Spirit. Evangelism is about obeying and then letting go, trusting God to fulfill God's purposes. God consecrates us for mission as we worship, and then God consecrates those we evangelize to become disciples of Jesus Christ.

First Church deployed this logic. After having prayed about the young adults' request, a small group of members worked with the young adults and the pastor to create worship in the pub. They spoke with the pub owner who was happy to help them if they met at a time when the pub was not packed with people. The owner figured anything that could potentially attract more regular customers, especially when the bar was not that full, was a positive.

They then discussed what worshiping in a way that was authentic both to the mission of God and to how the young adults related to one another would look like. In doing this, the First Church folks had to swallow hard and listen as their assumptions about what worship included, such as hymnals, a twenty-minute sermon, and a specific structure of leadership and liturgy, all dissipated. New ideas, like using smartphones during worship both for content and to share what was happening on social media, got introduced.

The people of First Church knew this new pub worship was not something most of them would ever want to attend, but they also recognized that they were not working on a new kind of church for themselves. They were there to legitimize the young adults in claiming the Christian faith. They served as guides to help the young adults develop a way they could be consecrated by God through worship. Based on that, they hung in there, praying for the endeavor while not always quite understanding what was happening. After a couple of months, FPC (First Pub Church) launched with about a dozen people in attendance. They still saw themselves as a part of First Church, but the young adults had forged a way to worship all their own. Both the congregation at First Church and the congregation at FPC knew they would have to work out details for how to relate to each other. For the moment, though, they felt they had seen God work to make disciples after they had obediently taken a step into the unknown.

Key Tactics: How to Seek Consecration in Worship

- The personnel committee should vet worship leaders, including the pastor, for how they personally live holy lives.
- The personnel committee should provide for ways to encourage leaders, including the pastor, to be encouraged in holy living. This could be through making time for them to participate in small groups, go on retreats, or share their personal stories about their devotional lives.
- Worship should avoid being a service provided by professionals for the consumption of people who attend.
- Worship should focus on inviting people to encounter God in order that they can be consecrated for holy living; and, in turn, be more effective in inviting people to become disciples of Jesus Christ.
- Worship leaders should develop ways of measuring worship that consider how it affects the way people are living.
- A congregation should decide what language, symbols, traditions, and rituals it uses in worship based on what aids the congregation best in coming into the presence of God.
- People in the congregation should be appointed to help the visitors understand anything that might be strange to those unfamiliar with the church.
- Worship leaders should remain open to changes in the practice of worship, both in planning and in the actual times of worship. If you discern God calling you to do something different, you should be willing to abandon your original plans and do that.
- While there is no problem with having a standard order of worship, the congregation should be taught that the order only facilitates worship. It does not define it.

- Worship leaders should be open to new times and practices of worship that will better facilitate new groups of people entering the presence of God and being consecrated for mission. This can include a worship time geared more for people unfamiliar with church and a worship time for those who are already disciples. In all cases, a worship time for existing disciples is essential.
- The congregation should be taught that evangelism is related to worship, in that Christians look to meet God in the process of both activities.
- People in the congregation should share stories with each other of how God has moved in power to support them after they have been obedient.
- People in the congregation should look for opportunities to meet with people who visit during worship, such as over coffee and snacks when worship is completed. Make sure there are ways to follow up with those who want to grow in their faith based on what they experienced in worship.
- The pastor or other designated people from the congregation should follow up with those who visit worship for the first time. Use pew pads or other means of gathering their information, and then contact them the following week.

CHAPTER FOUR

STANDING FIRM

Nehemiah 6:10-14

The camera pans over a large arena, packed with a roaring crowd. As its shot tightens, we can see the officials in their booth and feel the crackle of excitement coming from the people in the stands. The spectacle is about to begin, as both the saints and lions prepare to take the field.

This is no football game, however. It is the year 155, and the Roman persecution of Christians is in full swing. Just a few days before, a group of Christians had been torn to pieces by wild animals after having been placed on beds of spikes, flogged so badly that their organs were visible, and burned. Incited to a greater bloodlust by these antics, the crowd called for the bishop to be located and executed.

Elderly Bishop Polycarp was hunted down and brought before the governor in the arena. *The Martyrdom of Polycarp*, an ancient Christian text, describes what happened next:

> Thinking an old man would want to avoid dying in agony, the governor "sought to persuade him to deny [Christ]." ... "Swear [by Caesar], and I will set thee at liberty, reproach Christ;" Polycarp declared, "Eighty and six years have I served Him, and He never did me any injury:

how then can I blaspheme my King and my Saviour? . . .
hear me declare with boldness, I am a Christian.'"[1]

The martyrs are the most powerful example we have of being a public witness for Jesus Christ. Their witness was so powerful that it drew many people to become disciples. As Tertullian put it, "the blood of Christians is seed," sometimes translated as "the blood of the martyrs is the seed of the Church."[2]

As powerful as their witness was, the martyrs did not seek martyrdom. The early Christians believed that only the foolish chased after becoming martyrs. Even Bishop Polycarp hid when the Romans first began looking for him and only gave himself up when it became clear there was no way to escape. Rather, people became martyrs when they had no choice but to stand fast in the face of persecution. When placed in this position, martyrdom was how they participated in God's mission of making disciples.

While retreating from the public eye during evil times can be a good missional tactic, there are times we must remain publicly engaged and stand unmoved in the face of danger. For the martyrs to have backed away when challenged to renounce their faith would have been to impugn their witness and to suggest that God was ultimately untrustworthy. They would not do this.

Like the martyrs, sometimes to be in mission requires us to stand still, so we can be public witnesses to our trust that God will sustain us even in difficult times. In those moments, we have not only the martyrs but Jesus as our companion.

Jesus set the example for standing firm in his public mission when confronted by evil. In one situation, he was warned to leave a certain region because Herod was looking to kill him. His response was to stay the course of his public ministry, refusing to be afraid

---

1 "Encyclical Epistle of the Church at Smyrna Concerning the Martyrdom of the Holy Polycarp," chaps. 9–10, translated in *Ante-Nicene Fathers* vol. 1, eds. Alexander Roberts and James Donaldson (Peabody, MA: Hendrickson Publishers, 1994; repr. from Christian Literature Publishing, 1885), 41.

2 Tertullian, "Apology," chap. 50, translated in *Ante-Nicene Fathers* vol. 3, eds. Alexander Roberts and James Donaldson (Peabody, MA: Hendrickson Publishers, 1994; repr. from Christian Literature Publishing, 1885), 55.

of what Herod would do (Luke 13:31-33). Better known and more pointed was how Jesus withstood the trials and interrogations after he was arrested. When confronted by the members of the Sanhedrin and by Pilate, he refused to give an inch. He did this by remaining silent as his accusers attempted to pin him with various crimes (Matt 27:14; Luke 23:9; John 19:9). In doing this, he changed the power dynamic of the situation. He did not allow his accusers to have complete power over him but asserted that there was a greater power he trusted. He made this point to Pilate in the Gospel of John: "Pilate therefore said to him, 'Do you refuse to speak to me? Do you not know that I have power to release you, and power to crucify you?' Jesus answered him, 'You would have no power over me unless it had been given you from above.'" (19:10-11).

Unlike the times when Jesus retreated in prayer, these times of standing firm required that he remain in the public eye as a witness for the kingdom of God. To go into hiding just prior to his journey to Jerusalem because of Herod's threats or to take advantage of Pilate's discomfort with the accusations brought against him so that he could be released would have been contrary to the mission God had given him. To fulfill his mission required him to be unmoved in the face of opposition, taking whatever pain might come from it.

The book of Hebrews tells us that persevering as a public witness when facing difficulties was not new with Jesus. God's people had been doing this over the centuries. Hebrews 11 especially reminds us of many people who stood firm when confronted with suffering and death so that they would be faithful participants in God's mission. The Bible makes it clear that God honors these people. Moreover, their witness was successful in that we still know their names and beliefs while the names and causes of their persecutors are lost in history.

When Opposition Arises

First Church had been moving along relatively well since the establishment of FPC. There had been some dissatisfaction with First Church being related to a pub, and a few people had left First Church over it. There were also some people in the town who continued to look at First Church uncharitably for its connection to the musician who had been convicted of child abuse. However, the congregation's work with the residents of the Hispanic neighborhood largely overshadowed that negativity. The pastor had even said in a sermon that it seemed that everything would be quiet for a while.

As it turned out, "for a while" lasted only a few weeks.

One evening the pastor got a call from the district superintendent saying that the bishop had been impressed with how First Church had progressed through its recent difficulties. The bishop had a larger church in the city that could benefit from this pastor's gifts, and so the bishop was reappointing the pastor to the city church in three months. A new pastor would be sent to First Church.

The people at First Church were not happy to lose their pastor. Many felt as if this turn of events fell into the category of "let no good deed go unpunished." After the people of First Church had struggled, the denomination was taking away a pastor who had been instrumental in helping them find a level of stability and missional activity they had never known. This upcoming transition was hard enough, but it became even more complicated when the congregation was introduced to its new pastor—a Hispanic woman.

Over its entire history, First Church had been an almost entirely white congregation in an almost entirely white part of town. While neither the people of the congregation nor the town had seen themselves as hostile to nonwhites or as racist, they also had not seen the difficulties faced by those of other races. Their lack of awareness about the Hispanic population in the neighborhood where First Church was now doing ministry was a perfect example of this. The idea that public funding or business investment could be linked to discrimination had never dawned on them.

While the congregation's social consciousness had been growing so that they understood how advocating on behalf of those in need was part of God's mission, the idea of being led by a Hispanic woman required more of a stretch. It was one thing to care for people in another neighborhood or even to speak alongside them at city hall. It was even fine to welcome them as guests into the church. But to break down the last bastion of separation by having a Hispanic woman as their leader was no easy thing.

Several people at First Church aired their reservations to the personnel committee, asking if it would be possible to negotiate a different appointment with the bishop. The members of the committee were sympathetic and promised to consider the matter carefully. Having listened patiently to the people in the congregation, the committee members avoided making any hasty decisions. Instead, they prayed.

From the time they had faced the financial difficulties, the committees at First Church had continued their practice of prayer. And so the personnel committee was already well accustomed to praying about their business as they sought God's help to make sense of the pastoral change. Over the course of the next two months, many of the people on the personnel committee found they were being drawn to the psalms in their personal Bible reading, especially those in which the psalmist recounted how God had been faithful to the people of Israel throughout its history. The committee members could not avoid connecting this to how they had experienced God's provisions over the past several months in the face of several major problems. Based on this, their trust was strengthened, believing that God would not abandon them now. In addition, they began to develop a sense that this new pastor was going to be God's agent for leading the congregation to participate in God's mission in new ways.

The personnel committee shared this with the people in the congregation and enjoined the congregation to pray together for the ways the new pastor might lead them. The outgoing pastor even focused his sermons on the psalms to help set the stage for the new pastor. Thus, while the congregation still had doubts and anxiety, it was largely excited about what God would do through the ministry of the new pastor.

At the same time the congregation was praying and reading the psalms, the word that a Hispanic woman would be arriving as the pastor of First Church had made its way into the community. The initial discomfort felt by the people in the congregation was multiplied many times over in the town. The few naysayers in the town who still were angered by the congregation's past problems became vociferous, even writing comments on a local blog and sending letters to the local paper to state that First Church had been working to erode the fabric of the community. It had allowed child abuse and had advocated for town money to be siphoned away from the respectable neighborhoods to a crime-ridden neighborhood. Now First Church wanted to bring in a Hispanic leader. This was just an effort to further upset the economic and political stability of the town.

Even those who did not have such a negative view of the congregation were leery of the change. It did seem like First Church had been slowly but steadily drifting away from being a normal church. Why did they have to keep prodding the town to reexamine the status quo? Even the people who attended First Church were acting differently than they used to. They spoke more about their faith, and they openly talked about praying and waiting on God. They were not pushy or rude about it, but it was still a little jarring to hear these things in daily conversation from people they had known for years.

The people of First Church were surprised to hear all this. They folded these comments into their prayers, but they largely ignored them otherwise. They preferred not to prompt any further reaction by responding to the negative voices speaking about them.

That was until the night before the new pastor was to arrive at the church. The members of First Church had thought it would be a nice gesture to place a welcome message on their church sign, which faced the road. That way the pastor would see their welcome before she even turned into the church's parking lot. In the middle of the night, however, some of the people in the neighborhood decided that they wanted her to see a different message. As she and the congregation members arrived the next morning, they found the letters on the sign had been rearranged to make an ethnic slur with the additional comment "Go home!"

One day when I went into the house of Shemaiah son of Delaiah son of Mehetabel, who was confined to his house, he said, "Let us meet together in the house of God, within the temple, and let us close the doors of the temple, for they are coming to kill you; indeed, tonight they are coming to kill you." But I said, "Should a man like me run away? Would a man like me go into the temple to save his life? I will not go in!" Then I perceived and saw that God had not sent him at all, but he had pronounced the prophecy against me because Tobiah and Sanballat had hired him. He was hired for this purpose, to intimidate me and make me sin by acting in this way, and so they could give me a bad name, in order to taunt me. Remember Tobiah and Sanballat, O my God, according to these things that they did, and also the prophetess Noadiah and the rest of the prophets who wanted to make me afraid. (Neh 6:10-14)

The members of First Church were faced with a situation not unlike that of Nehemiah. Already engaged in important work that they believed was part of God's mission, both the people of First Church and Nehemiah were now dealing with angry outside sources that wanted to bring that work to an end. There was the potential of danger if they stood fast before this opposition. However, to back away would be to give up the powerful public witness that they had been developing.

Prior to this passage, Nehemiah had returned to Jerusalem and attracted the attention of the regional leaders Tobiah and Sanballat. They were opposed to Nehemiah's project of rebuilding the city walls. If the walls went up, the returned Jews could establish themselves as a political and economic force that would weaken Tobiah and Sanballat's control over the area. So they pressed Nehemiah to stop his work. When Nehemiah persisted, they sought to intimidate him with death threats, which is where we pick up the story in the above passage. In the passage, Nehemiah engaged in four important tactics related to standing firm in his mission:

1. He listened to what was going on around him.
2. He persevered in the work God had given him to do.
3. He discerned God's perspective on the situation.
4. He turned the situation over to God in prayer.

Listen

First, Nehemiah listened so he could become familiar with the situation around him. Nehemiah was no stranger to listening. The beginning of the book of Nehemiah says that he heard reports of the "great trouble and shame" that the residents of Jerusalem were enduring (1:3). This led him to risk asking King Artaxerxes for permission to go to Jerusalem and rebuild the city's wall.

Before Nehemiah arrived in the city, he met with the royal Persian officials in the region surrounding Jerusalem to determine how his work would be received. It was at this early point he learned about Sanballat and Tobiah (2:9-10). Following this, he made a secret inspection of the city, especially its broken walls, so that he would know just how big an undertaking rebuilding the walls would be (2:13). He continued to listen after he learned how dangerous Sanballat and Tobiah were. He routinely received reports about what they were thinking and modified his process of rebuilding the walls to counter the dangers they posed. Most of Nehemiah 4 describes how a network of people loyal to Nehemiah kept him up-to-date on what Sanballat and Tobiah might be planning and on how Nehemiah deployed his workers as both builders and soldiers to make certain the rebuilding continued unabated.

Nehemiah shows us that by listening to people where we are ministering, we become aware of issues that will directly affect how we carry out our mission of making disciples. This listening may sometimes force us to modify, speed up, or slow down our work, as Nehemiah did when he put half the workforce on guard duty while the other half rebuilt the wall, but that is not a problem. It is better for us to be aware of the full situation and respond wisely than to have our entire project destroyed because we wouldn't take the time to listen and learn.

There are numerous ways our congregations can listen. We can read the local newspapers and blogs. We can attend local meetings (for example, going to public meetings of the school board, city council, or county council). Most importantly, we can make a point of getting into the neighborhood and meeting people wherever they gather.

Most people are hungry to talk to whoever will listen to them. A local church-planting pastor demonstrated this with an experiment he conducted in a coffee shop. He sat down at a table and set up a sign that said, "I'll buy you a cup of coffee if you let me tell you my story." He sat for eight hours without a single person taking him up on the offer. The next day he returned and set up a new sign saying, "Buy me a cup of coffee, and I'll listen to your story." He had a line of people waiting to sit with him for most of the day.[3]

At the heart of all these possible ways to listen to our communities is making time to do it. Often this requires us to break our routine and seek opportunities to be with people. This does not mean forcing conversations where none are welcome. It means being open to conversations wherever they may happen. And, when they do happen, being ready to ask good questions and to listen to the answers.

Pastors especially need to take the lead in this, demonstrating that their job is to care for the entire area where they minister, not just the people inside the church building.[4] One pastor I know spent weeks literally walking through the town where she had just been appointed to find opportunities to speak with the people who lived there. This included taking her laundry to the local Laundromat, even though she had appliances at home, and chatting with any police officer or firefighter she saw. In addition, during a weekly dinner that her congregation served to the poor, she sat with the people at the table so she could eat and converse with them. Over several months she developed a good reputation with the people in her town, which blossomed into a far greater ministry for the congregation. She had listened to the people's stories and honored them. They responded by trusting her and accepting her ministry in their lives.

However, no one person can or should do all the listening for a congregation. All persons in the congregation can listen in the places where they are already living their daily lives, as well as by

---

3   Story from Curtis Brown, strategist—for the Western Jurisdiction for Path1, The United Methodist Church agency in charge of launching new congregations.

4   This is a key point in Dan Kimball, *They Like Jesus but Not the Church* (Grand Rapids: Zondervan, 2007), 36-49, 213-18.

making small modifications to connect with people outside their routines. If everyone in a congregation does this, the congregation will have excellent insight into the people they are inviting to be Christ's disciples. The importance of listening is doubled when our congregations face difficult situations. Like Nehemiah, we need to understand what is going on around us, so we can prepare an appropriate response to it. This leads us to the next tactic: persevering.

Persevering

Nehemiah knew God had commissioned him to build the wall. He made this clear when he first introduced the plan to rebuild, saying, "The God of heaven is the one who will give us success, and we his servants are going to start building" (Neh 2:20). Because of his faith that God would sustain him in this missional work, he was prepared to pursue it no matter what resistance came. This was essential, because he was well underway in constructing the wall around Jerusalem when he received the death threats. He would need his faith to persevere in his missional work.

Perseverance is not so much a tactic as it is a state of mind. However, there are tactics we can employ to help us persevere.

The first is to remind ourselves why we are doing what we are doing. Whatever our specific missional activity is, we need to remember that we are doing the work of God. This may seem an odd thing to say, but opposition can quickly seduce us into responding out of pride rather than out of God's strength. When we act out of our pride, we fall into a desire to compete with others. We feel as though we must either win or lose, kill or be killed. We emerge victorious over our opponents, or we meet an ignominious end with our opponent's foot on our neck. Given those options, we choose to fight or we run. Neither one is persevering.

Persevering is staying consistent in our work and standing firm in our convictions. It does not require us to defeat whoever is opposing us, it only requires that we do not buckle underneath their resistance. To do this, we need to remember why we are engaged in the work we are doing. We are not doing it for our own success or aggrandizement but to participate in God's mission in the world.

Since this is God's work, we can stand firm in our trust that God will not be hindered by any resistance we face.

A second tactic is similar: that we consider our public witness. How we respond to opposition demonstrates to those outside the church how genuine our faith is. If we respond with anger and a desire to crush our opponents, it will be clear to others that we are more interested in the success of our personal ventures than in the teachings of Jesus. What would the effect of the martyrs' public witness have been, for example, if they had come kicking and screaming into the coliseum, had been disrespectful to the governor, and had tried to fight the guards who held them? It would have been much different from how they submitted while still boldly proclaiming the good news of Jesus Christ.

One way to carry out this tactic is to use the "front-page test." This asks us to consider how our actions would be treated if they were reported on the front page of a major newspaper. What conclusions would the reporter draw about who we are and what we believe? What would the readers think about our presentation of the gospel? This is what Nehemiah did in verse 11 when he considered what it would look like if he, the governor of the Jews appointed by King Artaxerxes, ran and hid when he was threatened. He realized that if he did this, it would send a demoralizing message to his own followers and would communicate to his opponents how little he trusted God.

A final tactic for persevering is to make use of the gifts God has given us. As a congregation, we are made up of people with different God-given gifts. Paul explained, "Now there are varieties of gifts, but the same Spirit; and there are varieties of services, but the same Lord; and there are varieties of activities, but it is the same God who activates all of them in everyone. To each is given the manifestation of the Spirit for the common good" (1 Cor 12:4-7). Facing opposition does not change this. We can still use our gifts to persevere.

Nehemiah understood this. When he became aware of a military threat against Jerusalem, he found a way to have all the people persevere in their work: "From that day on, half of my servants worked on construction, and half held the spears, shields, bows, and body-armor; and the leaders posted themselves behind the whole house of Judah, who were building the wall" (Neh 4:16-17). By doing this, he gave each person a way to participate in the work according to their strengths while also dealing effectively with the threat hanging over them; those better suited to fight were placed on guard. Those who were better at construction continued to build the wall.

Although Nehemiah and his guards stood ready to fight, they did not invite a fight. Their purpose was God's purpose: to finish the wall. They just used their gifts differently to help the "whole house of Judah" to persevere in this work. This was not about prideful boasting of their military power. It was about mission.

Even though no attack came, the work of those standing guard is not denigrated or treated as less important than the work of the builders. If the guards had not been there, the builders would not have felt safe to use their gifts. Equal deployment of gifts does not mean that everyone will have equal activity or will be equally visible. Even so, all people are essential to carrying out the mission, and all should be honored for their service.

Congregations can likewise organize themselves to continue in mission by helping people discern their gifts and finding ways for them to use those gifts. In doing this, congregations should find ways to honor how everyone participates in the mission, not letting the honor go to just those who are most publicly visible because of their gifts.

Even the most physically feeble people have gifts for mission. Paul reminds us that ultimately, "Our struggle is not against enemies of blood and flesh, but against the rulers, against the authorities, against the cosmic powers of this present darkness, against the spiritual forces of evil in the heavenly places" (Eph 6:12). This means that we need people who will stand in prayer against these dark powers. Those who cannot physically participate in outreach events, advocate for just laws, or even get out of the house, can still be powerful guardians of the mission by their prayers on behalf of those who serve in these other ways. The physically weak should not be underestimated or forgotten as mighty protectors who can help a congregation persevere in God's mission of making disciples.

Discerning God's Perspective

It is always dangerous to suggest that we can see things the same way God does. God has a far broader and deeper view of the world than we ever can. However, that does not mean that we are entirely ignorant of God's perspective. As we have seen throughout this book, it is possible for us to discern what God's mission is and how we can best participate in it. Nehemiah was certainly clear about God's mission for him and the people of Jerusalem. However, this discernment can be much harder for us when we are suffering, especially when that suffering is caused because we are engaged in God's mission. Why does God allow us to suffer when we are faithfully carrying out God's purposes? Shouldn't God be protecting us?

First, God does protect us. One of the things God's grace does is to protect us from dangers that we never knew were dangers. This is one reason John Wesley sometimes referred to grace as "preventing grace."[5] Part of God's grace is to make it possible for us to accomplish God's will by preventing those dangers that would bring an end to our public witness completely. Because we were never aware those dangers existed, we don't recognize God's protection. We don't realize we have been spared.

This does not mean that God prevents all suffering for us. God sometimes uses these sufferings to heighten our public witness. The fact that Nehemiah persevered through the death threats generated greater credibility for his work among the people. They could see he was willing to sacrifice personally for it, and they responded in like kind by sacrificially giving of their time and safety to keep building the wall.

Nehemiah did not initially see how his perseverance increased his witness. Notice 6:12: "*Then* I perceived . . . " (emphasis added). It was only after he persevered that he realized why God allowed him to face persecution. The goal of his foes was to get him to lose

---

5   Scott Kisker, "Doctrines of Salvation: Preliminaries," *Methodist Doctrine* (Washington, DC: Wesley Ministry Network, 2010), DVD.

the credibility he needed to accomplish the work God had given him. God's goal was to increase his credibility by showing the people how committed he was to the mission.

Coming to these realizations requires patience. We rarely see the reasons behind the suffering while we face it. However, if we persevere with patience, we will have some of our questions answered in time. As we learn in Ecclesiastes 2:26 "For to the one who pleases him God gives wisdom and knowledge." However, if we grow impatient and refuse to persevere because we are embittered by our lack of understanding, we will both fail in God's mission and never receive the wisdom we are so desperate to have. The second half of Ecclesiastes 2:26 makes this clear: "but to the sinner [God] gives the work of gathering and heaping, only to give to one who pleases God." What we did accomplish for God's purposes will be handed to another. God's mission will go on, just without us, and we will be left without either purpose or answers.

Having a group of people hold us accountable is essential to developing this patience. These people also need to be committed to God's mission, so they can help us hang on when we feel overwhelmed. They can listen to us when we need to vent, pray for us when we have no voice to speak to God ourselves, and counsel us when we are lost in our struggles. By drawing from their strength, we have much deeper reserves with which to persevere in patience.

Nehemiah knew the importance of having this kind of support. In Nehemiah 5:17 he wrote, "There were at my table one hundred fifty people, Jews and officials, besides those who came to us from the nations around us." Although he was the leader, he did not try to face his difficulties alone. Nehemiah's example is important for how we understand the role of the pastor and laity in congregations today. The pastor should not just lead, but rely on the congregation for its support. Likewise, the congregation must not passively follow but step forward as participants in carrying out the mission of God alongside the pastor. This will strengthen everyone.

Turning It Over to God

Having gained clarity, Nehemiah turned the situation over to God. This is clear in 6:14 when he shifted from narrating his story to offering a prayer, asking God to see what happened and to deal with the people involved. Human pride is easily wounded and stirred up against the people who cause those wounds. It would have been easy for Nehemiah to bear a grudge against Sanballat, Tobiah, and the others who worked with them. Instead, he yielded them up to God in prayer. He may not have been ready to forgive them at this point, fresh from hearing their death threats against him, but his asking God to deal with them was a critical step in that direction. It was far better than harboring bitterness and revenge fantasies. In doing this, Nehemiah anticipated what Jesus later commanded: "love your enemies and pray for those who persecute you" (Matt 5:44).

If we do not pray for those who harm us, our lingering anger and pain will eat at our souls. This will suck our attention and energy away from our missional work. If left unchecked, it can be just as damaging to our public witness as if we had given in to our opponents, because the disgust we show toward those who harmed us will prove we are hypocrites who do not want others to share in the salvation offered by Jesus Christ.

Beginning a New Chapter

The first thing the new pastor and congregation members did after arriving on the pastor's first Sunday was to take a picture of the church sign with the slur on it, and then rearrange the letters back to the original message of welcome. The members of the congregation were quick to apologize to the new pastor for the offensive message and to assure her she was welcome. They joined together to pray about the incident and to seek God's blessing on the pastor's ministry at First Church, as well as to seek God's redemption for those who had vandalized the sign.

Both the pastor and the members assumed that after this first act of hate, the people in the town who were against a Hispanic pastor at First Church would leave the church alone. Unfortunately, they were wrong. When the congregation exited worship that Sunday morning, they found the sign had been changed again to display several ethnic slurs. They were shocked and appalled that someone would have done that while the people were worshiping. Uncertain of what to do, they took a picture again and removed all the lettering from the sign.

For some congregants, it was enough to do this. However, the leaders of the congregation felt compelled to give up their Sunday plans, pray with the pastor, and consider next steps. They prayed and fasted that afternoon, seeking God's will.

After three hours in prayer and discussion, a sense of unity came to the leadership. They remembered the work they had done to prepare for accepting their new pastor. They believed that she would be God's agent to help them forward in their commitment to God's mission. Assured in this, they decided they would not allow the acts of hate they had experienced to go unnoticed. They would use them to push forward in redemptive work that clearly needed to be done in the town.

The pastor e-mailed the two photos of the vandalized sign to the local online and print news outlets along with a brief statement saying that the pastor and leadership of First Church would hold a news conference to discuss the situation later in the week. Within twenty-four hours, the pastor had several local reporters contact her as well as a few reporters from larger news outlets in the state. They were interested in what happened and confirmed they would come to the news conference for more information.

In the days before the news conference, the church did a few other things:

- The leadership thought carefully about what they wanted to say, so they would have a simple, clear, consistent, and faithful message to share with the media.
- The trustees upgraded their sign, so it could not be rearranged unless someone had a key to it. They then used the sign to offer messages that spoke directly to the town. The first week, the message read, "God welcomes all. We do too."

- The pastor and other First Church leaders met with both the members of the Pub Church and the leaders from the Hispanic neighborhood where First Church had been working. In both cases, they explained the situation and asked for prayers and support in speaking to the media.
- The members of the Pub Church quickly began to use social media to generate support for First Church's effort to stand against racism and anti-immigrant sentiments using the hashtag "welcome2fc" (for "welcome to First Church"). They routinely tagged many of the media outlets to make their campaign more visible.
- The pastor and church leaders scheduled an appointment with the town mayor. Given the situation, the mayor made time in her schedule to meet with the First Church delegation. It was a brief meeting, but it gave a chance for them to become better acquainted and to discuss the need for dealing with the racism in their town.
- The pastor contacted the bishop and sought help from the denomination in terms of training and any other support available to navigate the road ahead for First Church.

By the morning of the news conference, there was a strong buzz about what the pastor and leadership would say. There was also new vandalism on the sign, this time in spray paint. There was no time to clean the sign before the news conference, but that ended up being a powerful witness to the words the pastor would speak.

Several people from the church, from the Pub Church, and from the Hispanic neighborhood attended the conference. A few people from the town came to stand against the hateful message written on the church sign even though they were neither members of First Church nor Christians.

During the news conference, the pastor explained that the desire of First Church was for all people to experience the love of God and become disciples of Jesus, living holy lives. She further explained that First Church believed part of living a holy life is to share God's love with others and to overturn any situations in which that love was being resisted or withheld. To put these beliefs into practice, First Church was ready to work with the mayor and other officials to lead conversations about racism and immigration in the town. Everyone would be welcome to these conversations. The pastor hoped that both town policies and the attitudes that had given rise to those policies would be discussed.

At the end of the news conference, the pastor invited all in attendance to a time of prayer. In the prayer, she lifted up not only this new endeavor to break the effect of racism on the town but also the people who were racist. She prayed for them to see that God loved them unconditionally, and by receiving that love they would be able to love others. She prayed that God would prompt them to come to the meetings being planned and that God would also allow them to meet and build relationships with people of other races. She prayed God would heal them even as God healed the town of its racist past and healed those being harmed by that racism, especially those in the Hispanic community.

This launched First Church unexpectedly into a new chapter of missional activity. That should not have been surprising, but it often is for those of us who think in terms of completing projects and meeting deadlines. Obeying the Great Commission has no end this side of eternity. Even when we think we have navigated successfully through certain situations, there is always more to do: more people to invite to become disciples, more opportunities to teach the ways of Jesus, and more situations in which we can be witnesses to the good news of what God has done through Jesus Christ in the power of the Holy Spirit.

This was true for Nehemiah. He did complete the wall, but once it was in place he had to turn his attention to ordering Jerusalem in new ways. The mission continued.

First Church had trusted God would continue guiding them in

mission with their new pastor. Having persevered in that trust, they realized that the new pastor coming and the opposition they faced with her appointment was God's way of revealing God's next steps for them in mission. They needed to move beyond the volunteering they had been doing and to make a clear public stand on behalf of God's redeeming love through Jesus Christ.

Key Tactics: How to Stand Firm in the Face of Opposition

- Listen to what is happening in your context. Be ready to change how you are engaging in mission based on what you hear.
- Modify your routine to connect to more people throughout the day. Take time to listen to what they say.
- Support pastors in caring for the people in the community as well as the people in the congregation. This should include expecting pastors to spend time in the community as part of their regular work.
- Develop a way for people in the congregation to attend public meetings and to report items the congregation can pray about or connect with in ministry.
- Remember that the mission belongs to God, and God will complete it.
- Avoid competing with people or engaging in "fight or flight" thinking.
- Use the "front page test" to determine whether the way that your congregation is handling its mission, especially any hostility it faces, is presenting a faithful witness to the teachings of Jesus Christ.
- Discern the gifts God has given each person in the congregation and deploy them in serving the mission.
- Honor everyone who serves, even those who are not visible in the work.
- Invite everyone in the congregation to be part of the mission, including the physically weak. Everyone is needed to seek God's power and protection in prayer.
- Be patient in suffering. It is OK to have questions

about why God allows us to suffer while we are faithful in mission. The answers often come only after we
persevere.

- Form small groups of people who can support each
  other, hold each other accountable, and encourage
  each other in mission.
- Create the capacity for the pastor and laity to share
  the mission and support each other rather than just
  seeing the pastor as the provider and the laity as
  receivers.
- Pray for those who harm you.
- Look for new opportunities to proclaim the love of
  God through Jesus Christ that arise out of the opposition you face.
- Make use of public spaces to share your message (for
  example, media, municipal offices, social media), especially if God prompts you to be a witness in a way
  that has implications for the public good.
- Keep the name of Jesus forefront. It is essential that
  people know the church is a witness for Jesus that is
  inviting people to become disciples, not just an institution that wants to do good things for others.

AVOIDING THE EXILE

Isaiah 2:10, 5:13; Jeremiah 20:6
Ezekiel 12:4; Nahum 3:11

The existence of refugees is one of the most poignant examples of how broken the world is today. News cameras linger on the weary and frightened faces of young parents with their wide-eyed children streaming out of war-torn regions to places where they hope they can find a better life. Desperate and destitute, they wonder if they can find their way to a stable home again.

Sadly, the world has almost never been without refugees. Even in the Bible we read about entire nations being uprooted because of violent and cruel invading armies.

By definition, refugees are innocent bystanders, caught in the conflict of military powers. They were rendered homeless and citizenship-less because of unbearable violence driving them away from the places where they had made their lives. They are among the "least of these" Jesus called us to care for in his name. Jesus even suggests that our faithfulness to him will be determined based on how we have treated such as these (Matt 25:40, 45).

There are other people the Bible speaks of who look like refugees but who are not innocent: those God sent into exile. These were people who lived in nations God judged to be wicked. As punishment, God brought powerful armies to uproot them from their homes. Most famously, the Bible describes how in 587 BC

71

God allowed King Nebuchadnezzar of Babylon to break through the walls of Jerusalem and take the city's inhabitants into exile:

> The LORD, the God of their ancestors, sent persistently to them by his messengers, because he had compassion on his people and on his dwelling place; but they kept mocking the messengers of God, despising his words, and scoffing at his prophets, until the wrath of the LORD against his people became so great that there was no remedy. Therefore, he brought up against them the king of the Chaldeans, who killed their youths with the sword in the house of their sanctuary, and had no compassion on young man or young woman, the aged or the feeble; he gave them all into his hand. All the vessels of the house of God, large and small, and the treasures of the house of the LORD, and the treasures of the king and of his officials, all these he brought to Babylon. They burned the house of God, broke down the wall of Jerusalem, burned all its palaces with fire, and destroyed all its precious vessels. He took into exile in Babylon those who had escaped from the sword, and they became servants to him and to his sons. (2 Chron 36:15-20)

Exile would appear to be the ultimate failure of mission. It is God's judgment against God's own people who were supposed to be in mission but who refused to listen to God's word. This is a dire situation. Yet it is one we need to contend with, since there are some scholars who suggest that exile is the best biblical image to understand the church in North America today.[1] If that is correct, it leaves us with serious questions: Is exile the end of mission? Would God allow for us to be in mission after such a severe divine penalty?

The good news for us is that God's discipline is redemptive, offering us a way to grow in grace and an opportunity to be a witness of God's goodness to others. Exile is God's way of forcing us to go to

---

1   Lee Beach, *The Church in Exile: Living in Hope After Christendom* (Downers Grove, IL: IVP, 2015). Joy J. Moore, "Pundits, Prophets, and Public Opinion," (sermon, Goodson Chapel, Duke University, Durham, NC, September 16, 2010), http://divinity.duke.edu/sites /divinity.duke.edu/files/documents/faculty-moore/pundits-prophets-public-opinion.pdf.

those who need to see the light of God when we have refused to go voluntarily. It strips away our comfort, brings us to repentance for our apathy, and leaves us with no other option except to live as the people of God among the people we avoided instead of calling into discipleship.

This was Paul's logic when he counseled the congregation in Corinth to excommunicate a member of the church who had an affair with his stepmother. Paul argued that such a life is utterly out of step with the teachings of Jesus. It was therefore a flagrant act against being a disciple. Even so, Paul did not suggest that the man was without hope, but he stated that the church should "hand this man over to Satan for the destruction of the flesh, so that his spirit may be saved in the day of the Lord" (1 Cor 5:5).

By expelling from the church those who do not conform to the teachings of Jesus, those who are not Christians see that the church takes God's mission to make disciples of Jesus Christ seriously. We will not brook hypocrisy within our ranks. Moreover, even the one expelled is given an opportunity to remain in mission. If he repents during his exile from the church, he can demonstrate to others what it means to sacrifice a life of sin to seek the holiness of God through Jesus Christ.

Exile, then, is not the end of mission. It is God forcing us to participate in God's mission after we have consistently refused to do so. When God sends us into exile, God is calling us to get busy doing the work of mission that we have neglected for too long. While we have reason to mourn and repent in exile, we do not have an excuse for not being a missional congregation.

Of course, even with that redemptive note, it is still better for us to avoid exile! In the case of First Church, the congregation had bypassed exile by engaging in the mission of making disciples intentionally. However, not everyone in the congregation was enthusiastic about the changes that action brought.

Resisting Mission

After First Church's pastor announced that the congregation would help lead conversations about racism in the town, there were about a dozen of the older members who felt as though the congregation had gone too far. They had already been unsettled by First Church lending its name to a group of people who met in the local pub and with the political advocacy that some of the members conducted on behalf of the Hispanic neighborhood. With the arrival of the new pastor and the news conference, they felt their congregation had lost its way. It had ceased to be a quiet town church where you could raise your family and learn about Jesus. Instead it had become an activist organization.

The members of this group had spoken with each other over the past year as these activities had unfolded around them. Now, on the Sunday following the press conference, they gathered to discuss their concerns and dissatisfaction openly. They told each other they just wanted to learn about God without all this superfluous activity connected to the congregation.

It was fine with them if some of the people in the congregation wanted to help those in need. They even were willing to accept a female Hispanic pastor. However, making First Church known for its political engagement was too much. This was not the kind of church they had known and supported all these years. Plus, attendance had not grown substantially since all this happened. The so-called "pub church" had been planted, but it barely contributed anything to the membership or treasury of First Church, so it was not like any of this missional work was beneficial to the congregation itself.

The group decided to talk with a long-standing church leader about this. This was the leader who had gone to the pub to meet the young adults for the first time. In the meeting, the leader admitted that he had been leery about the changes too. In fact, when the previous pastor had asked about going to the pub, he had serious reservations. He had even visited some other congregations and done a bit of hunting online to see what other options he might have for worship and church membership. He said that he was shocked by what he discovered. He found that many local churches in the United States were not faring well. Most had only around eighty people in attendance, and denominational churches were closing at an alarming rate. At the same time, churches that were serious about mission were opening and growing around the country. In fact, the very things that First Church was doing to cultivate its public witness were the things that made for a healthy church. They also provided a powerful reason for people outside the church to consider following Jesus Christ.

He said that after learning all this, he became convinced First Church was moving in the right direction. He added that, on a personal level, he had begun to recognize the presence of God in his daily life as he had become more intentional about prayer and sharing his faith with others. Even if this discontented group did not feel this way, he asked if they could support what First Church was doing because it was good for First Church. By being missional, First Church would likely continue to see at least modest growth and would remain an important organization in the town. After years of slow decline, wasn't this preferable?

The lay leader then explained that he felt First Church had developed some serious spiritual problems over the years without realizing it. They seemed so normal at the time; no one had noticed. However, with the insight the congregation had from seeking God and engaging in mission, they were becoming clearer to him and many of the other leaders. He offered these to the group as insight into where First Church might have been heading if it had not chosen the missional route that it did. We can use the lay leader's line of reasoning by considering those warning signs in our congregations.

> The word of the LORD came to me: Mortal, you are living in the midst of a rebellious house, who have eyes to see but do not see, who have ears to hear but do not hear; for they are a rebellious house. Therefore, mortal, prepare for yourself an exile's baggage, and go into exile by day in their sight; you shall go like an exile from your place to another place in their sight. Perhaps they will understand, though they are a rebellious house. You shall bring out your baggage by day in their sight, as baggage for exile; and you shall go out yourself at evening in their sight, as those do who go into exile. Dig through the wall in their sight, and carry the baggage through it. In their sight you shall lift the baggage on your shoulder, and carry it out in the dark; you

shall cover your face, so that you may not see the land; for
I have made you a sign for the house of Israel. (Ezek 12:1-6)

The passage from Ezekiel suggests that God warns those facing exile, giving them every opportunity to repent and support the mission of God. In this passage, God's warning to the people of Jerusalem was unmistakable. God had Ezekiel dress as an exile, pack up some meager belongings, and dig through the city wall to provide a dramatic enactment of what the people of Jerusalem would have to do when the Babylonians arrived.

The prophets give at least four major warning signs that God may send people into exile. We should take an honest look at our congregations to see if we encounter them. They are idolatry, self-centeredness, false teaching, and an emphasis on facilities.

As congregational leaders, we need to take this seriously. Do we discern God's warning? Is there danger that God has determined the only way to send our congregations into mission is to send them into exile because they are unwilling to go otherwise?

Idolatry

Their land is filled with silver and gold, and there is no end to their treasures; their land is filled with horses, and there is no end to their chariots. Their land is filled with idols; they bow down to the work of their hands, to what their own fingers have made. And so people are humbled, and everyone is brought low—do not forgive them! Enter into the rock, and hide in the dust from the terror of the LORD, and from the glory of his majesty. (Isa 2:7-10)

The primary reason the prophets give for God's people going into exile is idolatry. This may seem far removed from us today. There are few of us who are tempted to bow down before statues, hoping to receive blessings or avoid curses by doing so. However, the passage from Isaiah reminds us that idols are not always graven images but can be anything that is "the work of our hands" or what our "own fingers have made." This hits much closer to home.

Our chief idol is not a thing we might bow to but a perverse notion

of self-determination. Idolatry is giving way to the original temptation of the serpent in the garden, believing that we "will be like
God" (Gen 3:5), and therefore be able to operate apart from God.
We believe that we can chart our own destinies without any guidance from God because, as those who are like God, we do not need
or want an outside God telling us how to organize the universe.

The wealth we seek, the fame we desire, the innovative ideas we
want credit for, and the success we want to claim in all our endeavors: these are the manifestations of self-determination. Even giving
way to self-pity and a sense of having no self-worth is a manifestation of self-determination, since it argues that we can define ourselves apart from God. We can call ourselves worthless and failed
even if the Creator says we are "very good"(Gen 1:31).

This idol of self-determination is especially seductive to congregations. In a time when cultural forces press people to identify
themselves by where they stand on certain issues, congregations
can feel compelled to define themselves less by participating in the
mission of God and more by social, political, or economic agendas.
This confuses activity with identity. As we have seen in this book,
there are times when a congregation must engage in social, political, or economic causes. However, this work is an activity, not an
identity. Just because we do something does not mean that we become that thing. We are more than the sum of our activities.

When we treat our activities as our identity, we erode our missional call. A missional congregation recognizes this and refuses to
be defined as anything less than an agent of God's grace that demonstrates God's redemptive love through Jesus Christ in the power of
the Holy Spirit. When groups within the congregation start to push
for this identity to be merged with or defined by another agenda, the
leadership of the congregation needs to resist that.

Paul dealt with a form of self-determination in Galatians 3:27-28:
"As many of you as were baptized into Christ have clothed your-
selves with Christ. There is no longer Jew or Greek, there is no longer
slave or free, there is no longer male and female; for all of you are
one in Christ Jesus." In this passage, Paul pointed to how the idol of
self-determination can cause us to define ourselves by sociological or

cultural categories rather than by Christ. Paul is not suggesting that there are no longer differentiations in human society or culture but that we are no longer defined by those differences. Our identity is established by our baptism in Christ, not any social or cultural category.

This does not mean we ignore the social and cultural categories. These categories help us learn to relate to people better so we are more effective at inviting people to become disciples of Jesus Christ. As a simple example, I, as a middle-aged man, would share my faith with one of my young daughter's friends differently than she would. Where it would be perfectly appropriate for my daughter to hang out all day alone in her friend's room to talk, it would most certainly not be appropriate for me to do that!

The same thing applies to congregations. By comparing the demographics of the congregation to the demographics of the people whom the congregation wants to reach in mission, a congregation can develop a much more effective discipleship process. It is essential, for example, for ethnic churches to relate to those in their ethnic group through using the appropriate language, traditions, and rituals for that group. Doing this allows the congregation to share the teachings of Jesus in a meaningful way for people who share their ethnicity. Doing this does not mean that the congregation's ethnicity becomes equal to their baptism in defining their identity. Their identity should remain in Christ alone. It just means that their ethnicity is a gift God has given them to engage in mission more effectively with other people of the same ethnicity.

Nor does it mean that this ethnic congregation should only engage in ministry with those from the same ethnic group. The difference in ethnicity between the people in the congregation and those in the community around the congregation gives the congregation insight into how it can best position itself to relate to the people in the community. Just as foreign missionaries need to learn the culture and social structures of the country where they are going to live, so the ethnic congregation must learn the ways to invite those from the community to become disciples of Jesus Christ.

Accepting that our identity is defined by Christ overcomes our desire to self-determine through aligning ourselves with a specific group. Instead of making our allegiance to a group, we allow God to define us in Jesus Christ and reconceive the other categories as gifts to help us make disciples. In yielding both our identity and our relationships with certain groups of people to Christ, we avoid falling into the trap of idolatry.

The best way to tell if our congregations are infected with the sin of idolatry is to ask ourselves: What is nonnegotiable to our congregation? What can we not give up? If our answer is anything beyond our commitment to God through Jesus Christ in the power of the Holy Spirit, we must carefully consider whether we are pledging our allegiance to something alongside God. Can what we hold as essential be understood as a gift of God to serve in God's mission rather than as something that is equally important with God? If it can be, we should make certain we see it in its proper place; seeking only after God and God's kingdom, using the gifts God has given us to do this.

One way to determine what our congregation holds as essential to its identity is to look at what themes consistently return in how we teach our children and our new members. What beliefs and activities do we want to reinforce as essential for those who are young in the faith?

We can also determine our idols by thinking about whom we do not want to relate to in our congregations. We know from the Great Commission that Jesus will not reject anyone from being invited into discipleship. If there are people who we consistently think of as unwelcome in our congregation, that suggests we have lifted another commitment up to an equal level with our baptism, modifying whom we will evangelize based on the commands of our idol.

Self-Centeredness

Ah, you who join house to house, who add field to field, until there is room for no one but you, and you are left to live alone in the midst of the land! The LORD of hosts has sworn in my hearing: Surely many houses shall be desolate, large and beautiful houses, without inhabitant. For ten acres of vineyard shall yield but one bath, and a homer of seed shall yield a mere ephah. Ah, you who rise early in the morning in pursuit of strong drink, who linger in the evening to be inflamed by wine, whose feasts consist of lyre and harp, tambourine and flute and wine, but who do not regard the deeds of the LORD, or see the work of his hands! Therefore my people go into exile without knowledge; their nobles are dying of hunger, and their multitude is parched with thirst. (Isa 5:8-13)

The cry for justice is unrelenting in the world today. In relation to race, economic disparities, and many other issues, there are people who stand in need of being treated with basic human dignity, while those who could alleviate that suffering enjoy a life of excess.

There are few things that are as clear in the purposes of God than God's desire to bring justice. The prophets speak of it regularly. They condemn those who benefit at the expense of others and they paint beautiful pictures of God's shalom for those who honor God and neighbor (a state in which all people live in dignity and can flourish under God's gracious reign). Jesus stood in line with these prophets, calling us to love our neighbors as ourselves and to treat others as we want to be treated. When Jesus told us in the Great Commission that we should be "teaching [the nations] to obey everything that I have commanded you" (Matt 28:20) he expected us to include teaching about justice.

As clear as this call to justice is, there is a strong seduction to live comfortably and remain ignorant or apathetic toward the needs of others. It is easy for us to dedicate our time, energy, and other resources toward personal improvement and leisure, rationalizing that we deserve every good thing that comes our way. Congregations are no different from individuals in this. If we can raise a lot of money, increase our attendance, develop more small groups or classes, or generate any other positive numbers, we often feel as though we are doing everything we need to do for the mission of God. We can then reap our justly earned rewards.

This thinking runs afoul of God's call for justice. The church is not an end in itself. It is God's creation to carry out God's mission in the world. That means that individual congregations do not engage in ministry for their own numerical success but to participate in bringing about God's purposes. To miss this is to put ourselves in danger of exile, where God will strip away all the good things we are enjoying to force us to be in mission among those who cry out for justice.

This is the point Isaiah is making. Speaking to those who have increased their wealth by amassing land at the expense of others, Isaiah says that God will cause that land to decrease in its productivity. In doing this, God will remove the security that the people thought they had because of their land. No matter how much land they accrue, they will not be able to grow enough food. They will have vast landholdings, but they will still starve.

If the people continue to seek after their own comfort at the expense of others, God promises that exile awaits them. They will be afflicted with hunger and thirst just as the poor have been, and they will be forced away from the land they had coveted. By sending them into exile, God would force the formerly wealthy to live in solidarity with those who had suffered because of them. Since the wealthy had not shared with the poor, the wealthy will become poor and dependent on someone else to share with them.

Congregations can likewise be sent into exile by being forced into times of deficient finances and decreased attendance. Many of our mainline congregations remember the "golden years" when they had a large membership, were full of children and youth, and were flush with money. In many cases, our congregations used this largesse to care for those already inside the church rather than to obey Christ's command to make disciples by reaching to those outside the church. The result has been an exile of sorts. By relying on culture to give credibility to the church rather than the church seeking to influence culture, congregations began to lose members and dollars when the culture shifted away from supporting the church.

Aside from a few examples, the church in Western cultures is not seen as being allied with the interests of the poor. This lack of commitment to justice has left congregations struggling, especially at a time when people outside the church are interested in organizations that care for the needy.[2] Exiled from the center of Western culture, congregations are now scrambling to show they understand the need for justice.

Even in exile some of our congregations are content to hang on, waiting for the culture to shift back to the way things were instead of embracing the call to justice. They are still unaware of the injustices that need to be addressed and refuse to find small ways to advocate for those in need. Such congregations are in danger of being closed as God forces the people out of their comfortable enclave and into mission as individuals who need to grapple with the social ills around them without the support of the church.

Social Justice Handbook offers a series of steps congregations can take to promote justice as part of God's mission. These steps build on each other to move a congregation from "apathy to advocacy."[3]

- Praying to welcome God into the congregation, so we can see other people as God does.
- Becoming aware of the forms of injustice around us and focusing on a specific issue that we feel deeply convicted about changing.
- Lamenting for the loss experienced by victims of injustice.
- Repenting of our complicity in harming others (even if our complicity has been done in ignorance, not realizing that we were benefiting from something that was harming others).
- Seeking partnerships with those who desire to work for justice in the situation we have identified.
- Sacrificing whatever we must to engage in works of justice, including time, effort, resources, and the benefits we have accrued as a result of injustice.
- Advocating on behalf of those being treated unjustly

---

2   Bob Smietana, "Research: Unchurched Will Talk about Faith, Not Interested in Going to Church," LifeWay Research, June 28, 2016, http://lifewayresearch.com/2016/06/28/unchurched-will-talk-about-faith-not-interested-in-going-to-church/.

3   Mae Elise Cannon, *Social Justice Handbook* (Downers Grove, IL: IVP, 2009), 88–105.

in multiple ways: (a) spiritual advocacy by inter-
cessory prayer and fasting; (b) social advocacy by
seeking to persuade others about the importance
of rectifying the injustice; (c) legal advocacy by participating in the legal process of helping victims; (d)
political advocacy by engaging with governmental
structures to change systems that are unjust.

- Articulating that our advocacy is driven by our love of
  Christ so our public witness is clear.
- Celebrating the times when there are successes in
  overcoming injustice.

Our congregations support injustice either by actively depriving
others or by passively participating in situations that cause some
to benefit at the expense of others. We can only support justice by
being intentional in that work. If we fail to seek justice on behalf of
our neighbors, then God may send us into mission by being in exile.
We will either join in solidarity with those treated unjustly by giving
of ourselves on their behalf now, or we will join in solidarity with
them as exiles who are treated unjustly too.

False Teaching

Now the priest Pashhur son of Immer, who was chief officer
in the house of the LORD, heard Jeremiah prophesying these
things. Then Pashhur struck the prophet Jeremiah, and put
him in the stocks that were in the upper Benjamin Gate of
the house of the LORD. The next morning when Pashhur released Jeremiah from the stocks, Jeremiah said to him, The
LORD has named you not Pashhur but "Terror-all-around."
For thus says the LORD: I am making you a terror to yourself
and to all your friends; and they shall fall by the sword of
their enemies while you look on. And I will give all Judah
into the hand of the king of Babylon; he shall carry them
captive to Babylon, and shall kill them with the sword. I
will give all the wealth of this city, all its gains, all its prized
belongings, and all the treasures of the kings of Judah into

the hand of their enemies, who shall plunder them, and seize them, and carry them to Babylon. And you, Pashhur, and all who live in your house, shall go into captivity, and to Babylon you shall go; there you shall die, and there you shall be buried, you and all your friends, to whom you have prophesied falsely. (Jer 20:1-6)

The idea of heresy (the warping of Christian beliefs so they teach something other than what the church officially teaches in its doctrine) seems arcane and out of place today. The word summons notions of angry townsfolk holding witch hunts or Spanish inquisitors meting out punishment in medieval courts.

The notion of heresy is so distasteful that many mainline denominations opted to minimize holding people accountable to doctrinal standards in the early 1900s. The Methodist Episcopal Church, for example, decided in 1904 that bishops would no longer have the authority to inquire into the beliefs of theology professors who teach in the denomination's seminaries.

It is true that the desire to root out heresy has often bred cruelty, and the church is wise to repent of that. Such cruelty represents the worst of human nature and the opposite of God's love given through Jesus Christ.

While acknowledging the sins that have often attended efforts to stamp out heresy, the church cannot cede its responsibility to keep its teachings faithful to what God has revealed about who God is and how God acts. The need for faithful teaching is a consistent theme in the Bible, spanning both Old and New Testaments. Jeremiah, Ezekiel, Matthew, Mark, Luke, 2 Peter, and 1 John all warn against heeding teachers who speak in God's name but who do not speak what God has revealed. They also declare that God will bring wrath against teachers who do this.

In the passage above from Jeremiah, a priest named Pashhur heard Jeremiah delivering his warnings that Jerusalem would be overthrown and the people sent into exile. Angered by this, Pashhur publicly assaulted Jeremiah and had him thrown into the stocks overnight. Presumably, Pashhur believed and taught what other false prophets were teaching at the time: that God would spare the people of Jerusalem (Jer 6:13-14; 23:16-17).

When Pashhur released Jeremiah the next day, Jeremiah had a word from God specifically for him. Jeremiah said that Pashhur would be among the greatest examples of those who would suffer and be sent into exile. He would watch the destruction of his family and friends, as well as of his nation and the Temple. All the things he trusted would be secure would be crushed by God through the Babylonians. In this way, he would be a witness to God's faithful revelation. People would see his misery and know that God had spoken truly against him rather than through him.

This is an unhappy way to become a public witness; but for those who speak in God's name without being secured by the revelation of God, it is their lot. God will not allow people to be participants in God's mission on their own terms. For those who do this anyway by preaching their own message instead of a message God has authorized, God will make them witnesses in a different way. This often means sending them into exile as a sign of God refusing to be mocked.

It could be argued that we are already seeing this sort of exile within the American mainline church. Ed Stetzer, citing the General Social Survey, has reported a decrease in the percentage of Americans stating they are part of the Protestant mainline denominations from 28 percent in 1972 to 12.2 percent in 2014. Per Stetzer, one of the major reasons for this is a "lack of theological clarity."[4] This is a polite way of stating that mainline denominations in the United States have failed to preach the gospel clearly and faithfully. Could it be that the hemorrhage of members is God sending the members of these denominations into exile so they can be a public witness that God will not allow for such sloppy teaching in God's name? Stetzer hints at this when he concludes, "Research tells us that Convictional Christians are not leaving the faith. Instead, the 'squishy middle,' as I like to call it, is being compressed. At least part of this is because Christians now find themselves more and more on the margins in American society—not persecuted, but no

---

4   Ed Stetzer, "The State of the American Church: When Numbers Point to a New Reality," *Evangelical Missions Quarterly,* July 2016, https://emqonline.com/node/3520.

longer central. As such, people are beginning to count the cost."[5] Those who have not been committed to God's revelation, Stetzer's so-called "squishy middle," either must choose to become "convictional" by bringing their beliefs in line with God's revelation or go into exile from the church as a witness that God will not allow for slipshod theological teaching.

In Western cultures where we value freedom of belief, the idea of God requiring people to believe and teach in specific ways is offensive. Doesn't God want us to think carefully about what we believe, weighing the evidence we encounter and coming to intelligent conclusions? Yes, but this does not mean that because we decide something about God that we are necessarily right. When God met Moses at the burning bush, God responded to Moses' question about God's name by saying, "I AM WHO I AM," not "I am who you want me to be." God alone defines God. We do not. Our most carefully considered beliefs are of little meaning if we do not bring those beliefs in line with God's revelations to us.

God does care what we believe, and God will send into exile those who teach what is not in line with what God has revealed. In doing this, God makes such teachers a public witness to others that God's truth is not for humans to modify to fit our tastes. We must take God on God's own terms.

A critical tactic for our congregations is to identify what sources we believe are divine revelation. What do we think God uses to reveal information about who God is and what God does in the world? Is it the Bible, personal experience, something else? As an addendum to this, our congregations should be honest about how they interpret those sources. What lenses do we use to determine what God is saying and to apply those sayings to our lives today?[6]

A helpful tool for this reflection is the Wesleyan Quadrilateral.

---

5   Ibid.
6   This point opens the question of what God's revelation is. I address the importance of dealing with this issue for evangelism in my book *Evangelism for Non-Evangelists* (Downers Grove, IL: IVP, 2016), 52-58.

Developed by Albert Outler, a scholar of John Wesley, it states that the Bible is the primary source of divine revelation. We interpret the Bible by considering how the church has understood it in the past, our personal experiences, and our reason. This process grounds us in the unanimous belief of Christians throughout the centuries that the Bible holds a unique place as God's revelation to humanity, while taking our human contexts into account as we interpret that revelation.

Focused on Facilities

> You also will be drunken, you will go into hiding; you will seek a refuge from the enemy. All your fortresses are like fig trees with first-ripe figs—if shaken they fall into the mouth of the eater. Look at your troops: they are women in your midst. The gates of your land are wide open to your foes; fire has devoured the bars of your gates. Draw water for the siege, strengthen your forts; trample the clay, tread the mortar, take hold of the brick mold! There the fire will devour you, the sword will cut you off. It will devour you like the locust. (Nah 3:11-15)

Church buildings are more than just brick, mortar, wood, nails, and shingles. They are holy ground. Even though we know "the church" is the people of God, many of us were raised to associate the word *church* with a building. We "go to church" or we see "a church" on the street corner. We were likely also taught to think of that church building as "God's house." A church building demanded respect.

Church buildings are places where we mark critical passages in our lives. They are where we baptize, confirm, marry, bury, pray for the sick, and celebrate milestones. They are also where we may have felt the presence of God either directly or through the care we have received from God's people. For all these reasons, it is easy for congregations to feel a deep affection for their facilities. They are the physical manifestation of God's presence, the fortress to which we can return for calm and protection from the outside world, and an architecturally visible reminder in the community that the Christian faith is still alive and well in the neighborhood. It is little wonder that congregations often use pictures of their buildings as prominent features in their marketing and that congregations frequently spend a large portion of their resources on maintaining their buildings.

For all the benefits of having such a special congregational space, buildings can also be one of the greatest hindrances to congregations being in mission. Time, effort, and money that could be freed for engaging in mission go to sustaining the building. This is especially problematic for smaller congregations that are just making ends meet. The congregation begins to exist for the sake of keeping up the building as a monument to their faithfulness rather than the building being a tool that can be expended in the mission of God. For this reason, God may send us into exile to break our loyalty to our buildings and get us into mission.

In the passage from Nahum, the prophet mocks those who think they have constructed fortresses that can protect them against God's wrath. Nahum was writing specifically to the city of Nineveh, the powerful capital of the Assyrian Empire. His prophecies acknowledged that the Assyrians had conquered Thebes, Cush (present-day Ethiopia), and Egypt, even though their cities and fortifications had been formidable. Nineveh was supposedly greater than any of these conquered cities, a secure location from which the Assyrian kings could order the world around them. Yet Nahum claimed Nineveh would be overthrown easily. Nahum chided the Assyrians for putting their confidence in what they had built. He even taunted them to construct more impressive walls and defenses by making more bricks and providing for greater stores of water. None of this would matter, as God would smash it all. A force far greater than their buildings would come to crush them and send them out of their city.

The same can happen to us when we allow our facilities, not God's purposes, to become the primary beneficiary of our work and resources. No matter how much we may do to keep the building in good order, we can find ourselves being overthrown and sent into exile, so we can become missional by connecting with people in the community. God will remove us from our building if it is supporting our building that stops us from this missional work.

The only way to avoid going into exile from our buildings is to view our buildings as expendable resources God has given us for being in mission. This is painful for all the reasons we have discussed. It is hard to let go of a church building without feeling like a failure. Yet God's home is wherever God's people are. Remember, Jesus said, "Foxes have holes, and birds of the air have nests; but the Son of Man has nowhere to lay his head," (Matt 8:20). He also said "where two or three are gathered in my name, I am there among them" (Matt 18:20). In other words, Jesus never looked for a physical home on earth; he looked for a people who would gather in his name, and he made his home wherever they were. No building necessary.

For this reason, congregations should be willing to move their ministry beyond their buildings, even selling their buildings if the money they derive from the sale will be a better provision for staying faithful to God's mission. As uncomfortable a tactic as this might be, it is preferable to God "shaking" us out of our buildings because our loyalty was focused on them rather than on making disciples.

To take this step, congregations should connect with outside groups to help them assess whether their buildings are holding them back. In my own denomination of The United Methodist Church, Path1, a division of Discipleship Ministries that oversees church planting and revitalization, is an excellent resource for this.

For those congregations that can keep their buildings, they should commit to not overextending their resources in maintaining their facilities. Mike Slaughter, pastor of Ginghamsburg United Methodist Church in Ohio, offers one way of doing this. He recommends placing all congregational expenses into three large categories: mission, ministry, and mortar. *Mission* is everything the congregation does outside of itself to obey the Great Commission. *Ministry* is everything the congregation does internally to edify disciples. *Mortar* is everything relating to church property (maintenance, capital expenditures, insurance, and so on). He challenges congregations to keep their expenditures in mission higher than their expenditures in mortar.[7] By doing this, a congregation avoids making their facilities a hindrance to mission and a possible reason for exile.

Those Who Stay and Those Who Go

It is rare today for those of us in North America to be sent into exile in the sense of becoming refugees away from all we own and know. However, God could still be sending us into exile by denying us comfort. God could force us outside of a comfortable congregational setting and among those we were meant to be in mission to voluntarily. When exiled this way, we end up either being humbled, learning to be missional, and relearning what it means to be a church, or we become salt that loses its saltiness, worthless and fit for nothing. Either way we are witnesses for God, by finally participating in God's mission in the world or by demonstrating that God will not be mocked by those who want to claim the name of Jesus but not obey Jesus' commission. The discontented group from First Church fell into the second category. Their sin was especially around compromising with injustice toward others.

While the lay leader said he understood the group's feelings of discomfort, he also testified that he had become convinced God was moving First Church to live in greater solidarity with those who had less access to resources and opportunities in the town. This was not what the group wanted to hear. They wanted to hear that the old, inward-focused ministry the congregation had practiced for years was coming back. They wanted to hear that taking public stands on social issues on behalf of others was an innovation, a fad, something that could be easily dismissed as an unnecessary deviation from being a normal church.

Following their meeting with the lay leader, the group decided it was time to leave First Church. They wrote a letter to the pastor and lay leader saying that if the congregation was insistent on this new route, then it could go without them. They would take their money, time, and attendance elsewhere. They made it clear that they had been members of First Church for many years and that they hoped the

---

7   Mike Slaughter, *Change the World* (Nashville: Abingdon Press, 2010), 117–31.

congregational leaders realized they were alienating the people who had faithfully supported the congregation through its leanest times.

Initially, this group agreed among themselves to begin attending other congregations. After all, they were not abandoning their faith, they were sending a message to the leaders of First Church. In the Sundays after their departure, the group would meet at different congregations in the area for worship. They liked some of what they found, but inevitably they also found reasons they did not feel at home. These other congregations did not sing the right hymns or the sermons were too long or the ways they took Communion were foreign or the liturgies were unfamiliar.

Over those few weeks, members of this little group began to fall away from these excursions until the group had dissolved. A few settled somewhat discontentedly in other congregations, but many just chose to stay at home and talk about how congregations today were not as faithful as they used to be. They bitterly spoke of their own faithfulness and contrasted it to the anemic congregations around them, deciding they didn't need to attend a congregation since their faith was solid already. They also shrugged off any attempts that people from First Church made to invite them back. And so, they retired from being church members into obscurity and self-satisfaction. They had chosen to be in exile and never knew it.

Back at First Church, there was some trepidation because of the financial hit that the loss of these members would mean for the congregation. However, when the first month's numbers were run, the leadership realized that the people in the group had not been any of the major givers. Moreover, with their exit, the congregation found that they had a sweeter and more unanimous spirit as they gathered for worship, prayer, and administrative work. They felt more emboldened in their missional course, freed from those who had held on to the congregational sins that could have led to them all going into exile.

Key Tactics: How We Can Avoid Exile

- Ask what we value most in our congregations. If we find something we value equally with our identity as followers of Jesus Christ, we need to repent of that as an idol and either get rid of it or see it only as a tool for God's mission.

- Engage in justice. See the list from *Social Justice Handbook* in this chapter (see page 82–83) for several practices that move us from apathy to advocacy on behalf of the needy.
- Reject false teachings about God. We do this by articulating both the ways we believe God reveals God's nature and purposes to us and how we interpret those revelations. If what we believe sets us at odds with Christ's teachings or the mission to make disciples, we must repent of it.
- See our facilities as an expendable resource for engaging in God's mission. This means being open to renting, selling, or redesigning our buildings to better provide for the mission God has given us. It also means setting up a budget that gives mission precedence over facilities.
- Be willing to let people go. It is hard to lose church members, especially those who have been faithful for many years. However, if people remain obstinate by refusing to participate in mission, the congregation will not be able move ahead faithfully if it must stop and cater to them.

RECONCILE WITH EACH OTHER AND GOD

Matthew 5:24; Acts 6:1-7
Luke 12:58; 2 Corinthians 5:20

There are so many examples of brokenness that we could be excused for believing it is impossible for different groups of people to live together peacefully. The fault lines of race, political perspective, socioeconomic class, gender, and any number of other social categories seem to fester and give rise to ever-increasing violence. Alongside these are the hostilities that erupt between nations, tribes, and even family members. This results in people, especially children, being displaced, disregarded, abused, and killed.

Participating in God's mission includes working for reconciliation. Reconciliation, according to Brenda Salter McNeil, who has more than twenty-five years of experience in teaching reconciliation, "is an ongoing process involving forgiveness, repentance and justice that restores broken relationships and systems to reflect God's original intention for all creation to flourish."[1]

How can one local congregation bring reconciliation to a world shattered on so many levels? We can start by showing how Christians are a diverse-yet-reconciled people who can live with one another. In many ways, this is what the earliest church did in the book

---

1   Brenda Salter McNeil, *Roadmap to Reconciliation: Moving Communities into Unity, Wholeness and Justice* (Downers Grove, IL: IVP, 2015), 22.

of Acts. The church in Antioch, which launched Paul on his mission to the Gentiles, is the best example of this. Rev. Peter Hong of New Community Covenant Church in Chicago describes the church in Antioch as bewildering to the people outside of it.[2] In Acts 13:1, we are told that the leadership of the church consisted of "Barnabas, Simeon who was called Niger, Lucius of Cyrene, Manaen a member of the court of Herod the ruler, and Saul." These men were a diverse group. Barnabas was a wealthy man from Cyprus. Simeon was called "Niger," which means "black," leading many scholars to speculate that he was a dark-skinned man from Africa. Lucius was from Cyrene, a city on the northern coast of present-day Libya. Manaen, based on the Greek translated in this passage as "a member of the court," may have been raised as a childhood friend of Herod. Even if he was not, he was still a member of the nobility who worked closely with political rulers posing a serious threat to the church. Finally, Saul, later renamed Paul, was from Tarsus, which sat on the southern coast of present-day Turkey.

These men were from different places and would have been raised with different local languages, traditions, customs, and perspectives. These differences could have generated serious disagreements among them. Yet all of them were found praying together as brothers in the church at Antioch. It was during one of these prayers that God set aside Paul and Barnabas to become missionaries to the Gentiles, helping the Christian faith spread beyond its Jewish origin.

This diverse leadership is not surprising given how the church in Antioch was formed. Acts 11:20 says that the evangelists who first went to Antioch "spoke to the Hellenists also, proclaiming the Lord Jesus." *Hellenists* was a term used to describe anyone who was not Jewish, regardless of nationality, ethnicity, or skin color. The evangelists invited everyone to accept the gospel and become disciples.

The residents of Antioch had no capacity to understand what could draw such a diverse group of people together. Their only

---

2   Peter Hong, "Beyond Our Walls," Amplify Conference plenary session, August 24, 2016, https://www.youtube.com/watch?v=TOB89rL3l3c&index=14&list=PLxZddGvRSn2EPb-TGe9xmFcNLTWr4Y2T8.

experience of diversity came from the Roman Empire. The empire had a highly diverse populace, but it was held together by the threat of force if the various peoples did not live together in relative peace. What could the church's secret for voluntary multiethnic diversity be? Hong says the one thing that the diverse people in the church shared was their allegiance to Jesus Christ.[3] This was so obvious that the residents of Antioch named those in the church after Christ, using the term *Christian* in Antioch for the first time (Acts 11:26). What a remarkable public witness of how people from different backgrounds can be reconciled together as one in Christ! This experience likely prompted the verse 1 Peter 2:10: "Once you were not a people, / but now you are God's people."

It is not surprising that the church became a reconciler of races, ethnicities, and other differences so early in its existence. In the Great Commission, Jesus made it clear that God's purpose was for his followers to "go . . . and make disciples *of all nations*" (Matt 28:19, emphasis added). To be in mission is to reach out to all people. Jesus called for his followers to do more than teach different people how to obey his commands. He called on them to baptize those people. Baptism is the process of incorporating people into the community of God. It is the symbol of bringing people together as one reconciled community in the name of the Father, Son, and Holy Spirit.

However, reconciliation is not just a one-time act shown at baptism. The creation of a community requires an ongoing willingness of people to live with one another. This means regularly engaging in the practice of reconciliation by recognizing points of conflict in the community, repenting of wrongs done to one another, forgiving one another, and restoring relationships. All of this is part of the work of the Great Commission. This brings us back to our question: How can a congregation participate in God's mission of reconciliation, especially in situations in which deep animosity or mistrust already exists?

---

3   Ibid.

Reconciled with God

Even though the people at First Church had prayed through each step they had taken in mission, carefully weighing what they were doing, they had not expected events to develop as they did. Having committed themselves to help lead the town discussion on race relations, they felt utterly unprepared. They likewise felt that they could not just leave it to the pastor to carry the work. While she would be the most visible spokesperson for the congregation, everyone needed to support the process.

Compounding their sense of being unprepared was the opposition to these meetings. They had seen the anger in the town through the vandalism on their sign, and they had lost members who felt First Church was going down the wrong path by getting engaged in these meetings. This opposition made the congregation realize that it was not enough to take a stand for what they thought was part of God's purpose in the world by working to identify and eliminate racism. They also needed to work for reconciliation. They were concerned that to take a stand against racism without working to reconcile all people would generate greater anger in the town rather than allow them to share God's redemptive love through Jesus Christ.

In hopes of finding a way to promote reconciliation and gird themselves for the work before them, they turned to the Bible. The leaders of the church committed to pray and read passages that dealt with reconciliation. Over the course of the next few days, several of the leaders came across 2 Corinthians 5:11-21. This passage said the reason God sent Jesus Christ into the world was to reconcile all people to God. It also spoke of reconciliation as an essential aspect of the mission God had given the church. This provided the leaders of First Church a new framework to think about reconciliation. They saw that reconciliation does not start with how people relate to one another but with how God relates to people. True reconciliation provides people with a way to get right with God as well as to get right with each other.

The leaders asked the pastor to preach a series of sermons about this passage leading up to the meetings. She agreed, with the proviso that the congregation hold concurrent conversations about reconciliation in all the Sunday school classes and Bible studies, as well as in the ecumenical prayer breakfast the congregation continued to host. In addition, she asked that First Pub Church members have similar conversations, so everyone connected to First Church could be on the same page. The leaders agreed.

> Therefore, knowing the fear of the Lord, we try to persuade others; but we ourselves are well known to God, and I hope that we are also well known to your consciences. We are not commending ourselves to you again, but giving you an opportunity to boast about us, so that you may be able to answer those who boast in outward appearance and not in the heart. For if we are beside ourselves, it is for God; if we are in our right mind, it is for you. For the love of Christ urges us on, because we are convinced that one has died for all; therefore all have died. And he died for all, so that those who live might live no longer for themselves, but for him who died and was raised for them. From now on, therefore, we regard no one from a human point of view; even though we once knew Christ from a human point of view, we know him no longer in that way. So if anyone is in Christ, there is a new creation: everything old has passed away; see, everything has become new! All this is from God, who reconciled us to himself through Christ, and has given us the ministry of reconciliation; that is, in Christ God was reconciling the world to himself, not counting their trespasses against them, and entrusting the message of reconciliation to us. So we are ambassadors for Christ, since God is making his appeal through us; we entreat you on behalf of Christ, be reconciled to God. For our sake he made him to be sin who knew no sin, so that in him we might become the righteousness of God. (2 Cor 5:11-21)

This is a first step congregations can take to becoming agents of reconciliation: to learn about the topic of reconciliation in the Bible. The word *reconciliation* carries a great deal of freight because it sometimes gets attached to political and social agendas. When this happens, those who claim they want to reconcile draw a line in the sand that demands others acquiesce to their agenda rather than creating a space in which relationships can be restored through mutual listening and forgiveness. This usually ends with greater anger and disunity than what the group experienced before the conversation.

In the Bible, reconciliation does not conform to human agendas. Rather, it sets out God's cosmic agenda: to restore sinful humanity to a right relationship with its Creator. It is because Christians understand that God has reached out to restore this relationship through the death and resurrection of Jesus Christ that we have a powerful basis from which to work for reconciliation between people.

While related, there is an important difference in the reconciliation that Jesus Christ offers between people and God and the reconciliation he makes possible between different groups of people. This difference deals with the relative power of those who need to be reconciled and who needs to repent. In the case of reconciliation with God, while God is the most powerful party, only humans need to repent. In the case of different groups of people, usually both groups need to repent. However, there is a greater impetus for the more powerful group to repent since that group usually bears greater responsibility for the existing breach of relationship. Let's look at each of these reconciliations in more detail.

Even though God is the more powerful party compared to humans, God did not benefit from using that power to harm humans. Instead, God made humans in the image of God, allowing them freedom to choose how to live. Humans used their freedom to mar the image of God they carried, devaluing their own humanity through sin. To reconcile with God, then, is not a matter of setting right a wrong committed by a more powerful God against weaker humans. Rather, it is the process of God saving humans from exercising what power they had to reject the glory God had given them. God reconciles with humans by restoring humans to a right relationship with God, helping them past their sin to reclaim their place as the bearers of God's image.

God did this through sending Jesus of Nazareth who, as Philippians 2:6-8 puts it, "though he was in the form of God, did not regard equality with God as something to be exploited, but emptied himself, taking the form of a slave, being born in human likeness. And being found in human form, he humbled himself and became obedient to the point of death—even death on a cross."

Jesus set aside divine power and suffered as a human. He did this even though the breach in the relationship between God and humanity was caused entirely by humans. This is why the gospel is so remarkable. It tells us that God loves us enough to take the responsibility for our sin even though God did nothing wrong toward us. In doing this, God reconciles us and opens the door for us to share eternally in God's righteous life.

In recognizing this, the people of First Church came to realize that engaging in the work of reconciliation was an act of sharing the gospel. Just as the work of mission started by recognizing that God was already in mission as the sent God, so working for reconciliation came from recognizing that God began by reconciling humanity to a right relationship with God through Jesus Christ.

This was a good start. However, there are different dynamics involved when we apply God's reconciliation with humanity to how people reconcile with one another. The First Church leaders found this out as they worked to develop the town meetings on racial reconciliation.

Reconciled with One Another

When the pastor and others from First Church arrived at the first meeting, they felt more confident knowing that reconciliation was a work of God connected to the salvation offered through Jesus Christ. This meant that working for reconciliation was also working toward making disciples. In their prayers prior to the meeting, they asked that God would not only bring healing to the town but create opportunities to invite people into discipleship.

Even with this solid theological foundation, the people of First Church realized that reconciliation is not just a means of making disciples. Reconciling people who have been estranged is a worthwhile activity to pursue in its own right. It is worth our time, effort, and dedication to accomplish.

Most importantly, reconciliation requires all the parties who have been a part of the damaged relationship to participate. In the case of the town, reconciliation would not happen unless a cross section of people who lived in all the neighborhoods was involved. For this reason, people from First Church worked to make certain that residents of the Hispanic neighborhood as well as their own neighborhood attended. They wanted everyone's voice to be heard.

In addition, the congregation had asked the denomination for support. Even with their scriptural insight and prayer, they needed someone with expertise to help facilitate the meetings. Fortunately, their denomination had someone who could do this. After receiving the mayor's approval, First Church engaged this person. Prior to the first meeting, the mayor, the pastor, and several others from First Church met with the expert to make certain she understood the situation in the town.

About thirty people came to the first meeting. After initial remarks from the mayor and the pastor, the expert explained how the town had experienced an unexpected shock when the racist comments were placed on First Church's sign. She then explained how these meetings would not bring complete racial healing between the white and Hispanic communities in the town, but they were a step toward reconciliation through helping people in the town listen to each other and recognize how each experienced living in the town.

The expert had people sit in small groups at different tables and led them in decentering exercises. These were to help them become more open to the perspectives others would share. Then the expert asked the small groups to discuss what happened with the church sign.

What the people from First Church did not anticipate in the ensuing conversation was the amount of anger that residents of the Hispanic community presented. Hadn't First Church sacrificed to work in and advocate for their community? Hadn't First Church been involved consistently with the Hispanics for nearly a year now? Why were the residents of this community still voicing so much anger and hurt? This seemed to be a real lack of gratitude and acknowledgment for what First Church had done!

> So when you are offering your gift at the altar, if you remember that your brother or sister has something against you, leave your gift there before the altar and go; first be reconciled to your brother or sister, and then come and offer your gift. (Matt 5:23-24)

The passage from Matthew makes it clear that we cannot disregard what others say against us. Jesus does not say that if we have something against someone else we should leave the altar, but if we find that someone else has something against us it is more important to God that we make things right with that neighbor than it is for us to present our offering. We are called to "go; first be reconciled" as an act of mission.

This sort of reconciliation is often uncomfortable for us because it demands that we become vulnerable to someone else's perspectives. These perspectives cast us in a different light from the one we usually use to see ourselves. Unless we take the time to hear what the other person says and learn why he or she is saying it, though, there is no way for us to work toward reconciliation with that person.

This brings us back to the difference between how God reconciles with humanity and how people reconcile with each other. In the reconciliation between God and humanity, humanity harmed itself by misusing the freedom God gave it, but God opened the door for a repaired relationship through Jesus Christ. In this case, one side (humanity) was clearly in the wrong, the other side (God) was clearly innocent, and reconciliation involved restoring the innocence of the guilty party.

In reconciliation between people, all the groups are guilty on some level. Each has harmed the other. However, the harm is rarely equal. Usually, the more powerful party has benefited from allowing the weaker party to be kept weak. This means that, while the weaker party also has responsibility to work for a restored relationship between the two groups, the initial responsibility lay with the more powerful party to repent and seek forgiveness from the weaker party. A biblical example of this is Zacchaeus. When Jesus came to his house, Zacchaeus recognized he had misused his power as a tax collector and offered to refund those he had defrauded four times over and to give half his property to the poor (Luke 19:8).

The idea that the more powerful party needs to repent to move toward reconciliation is related to the notion of privilege. Privilege is when one group of people has more power simply because that is the way the culture and society have allowed things to be. In the case of Zacchaeus, he had more power because he chose to work for the Romans, giving him political and economic status over his fellow Jews.

Privilege is not always granted because of a job or political power. It can be based on social classifiers such as race, ethnicity, or gender. Today in the United States, for example, whites are often expected to have more wealth and influence than African Americans or Hispanics. It is true that many whites have worked for what they have, but cultural and social assumptions also gave them more opportunities to improve their quality of life as well as to pass that better quality of life from one generation to the next. An African American or Hispanic can work just as hard, and due to the cultural and social assumptions, not attain the same quality of life for themselves or their children.

What is difficult about privilege is that it seems to be natural. It is just the way cultural and social structures assume people will relate to one another. Certain people who attend certain schools or look certain ways or who live in certain neighborhoods are expected to be rich or poor, well educated and highly skilled or poorly educated and unemployable, capable of great things or of just barely getting by. Most people will tend to keep these assumptions in the back of their mind when they deal with someone, regardless of who that person is or how gifted that person is.

When we are privileged, we often do not know it until we have someone challenge us. And, for that challenge to make a difference, we need to listen. This listening is more than just a matter of decency. It is an act of mission. It is our way of being reconciled with others. The idea of adopting a listening posture when engaging in mission publicly may seem strange. We usually think of mission requiring us to take an active role in doing good for others or speaking our faith, not submitting to others who have something to say to us. We think of our inviting people to repent, not the other way around. Yet to be in mission through the work of reconciliation requires that kind of humility.

McNeil suggests that after experiencing a "catalytic event" that prompts us to seek reconciliation, we then must go through a process of realization, identification, preparation, and activation.[4] We realize that others have an alternative perspective from ours, we begin to identify with the pain others feel, we prepare to change how we live, and then we act together to advocate for greater justice. For those of us in privileged positions, this process requires us to keep our defenses down and listen well. Only when we do that will we be taken as serious as those who are on God's mission of reconciliation.

The Bible gives us an example of this in how the apostles responded to the complaints about the food distribution to widows:

> Now during those days, when the disciples were increasing in number, the Hellenists complained against the Hebrews because their widows were being neglected in the daily distribution of food. And the twelve called together the whole community of the disciples and said, "It is not right that we should neglect the word of God in order to wait on tables. Therefore, friends, select from among yourselves seven men of good standing, full of the Spirit and of wisdom, whom we may appoint to this task, while we, for our part, will devote ourselves to prayer and to serving the word." What they said pleased the whole community, and they chose Stephen, a man full of faith and the Holy Spirit,

---

4   McNeil, *Roadmap to Reconciliation*, 36.

> together with Philip, Prochorus, Nicanor, Timon, Parmenas,
> and Nicolaus, a proselyte of Antioch. They had these men
> stand before the apostles, who prayed and laid their hands
> on them. The word of God continued to spread; the num-
> ber of the disciples increased greatly in Jerusalem, and a
> great many of the priests became obedient to the faith.
> (Acts 6:1-7)

Most Christians at this point were still Jews from Judea. However, some adherents to the Jewish faith from the Greek-speaking areas of the Roman Empire also had been converted. The indication in this passage is that the Judean Jews (Hebrews) favored their widows over the Jews from the rest of the empire (Hellenists) when distributing food. This was an act of privilege.

To deal with this, the apostles needed to listen to what the Hellenists said. Then they needed to identify with the Hellenists, rather than treat them as a separate group from the main church, and prepare to do something. They did this by calling together the community where they acknowledged the complaint and laid out a plan that allowed for equality in the distribution of food. Finally, they acted by consecrating the new leadership to their task. In doing this, they reconciled the community from a serious breach, overcame the privilege being given to the Hebrews, and extended the mission of God in the process. The final verse suggests that God was pleased with this because God's power continued to be available to make disciples following this time of reconciliation.

This same process works, whether we are working for reconciliation inside or outside of the church. When seeking reconciliation for people in the context around us, congregations composed of people who are privileged must learn to listen without defensiveness if they are to be in mission. They must learn to hear the anger and frustration that other groups of people feel without trying to rationalize it away or distance themselves. Even if, as in the case with First Church, they have been working for justice, they still need to be ready to take a quiet, listening, and submissive posture. This is because the pain that other groups are sharing has taken generations to accumulate. Our months or even years of volunteering to make things better may ameliorate that a bit, but it does not come close to touching the depths of pain that the other group feels.

One way those of us who are privileged can take a submissive posture is by revisiting our testimonies of how God reconciled us through Jesus Christ. So often our testimonies are straightforward with a happy ending (I was a sinner, God saved me through Jesus Christ, now I look forward to glory). However, what happened is much more involved than that. We still have times of doubt, tragedy, struggle, and uncertainty. We still have times that we wonder whether God is there and loves us. Apart from being able to articulate these more ambiguous parts of our faith stories, it can be hard to listen to others who are in pain because we keep wanting to rush to a happy ending. The more honest we are about still working out our faith in God, the more we can be patient with the process of reconciling with others.

If congregations are made up of people who are not privileged, they should enter these conversations prepared to share their experiences honestly. It diminishes the process if the voices of those who have been harmed in the relationship are not clearly heard. This sharing may cause pain for the privileged groups to hear, but so long as the sharing is with the intention to reconcile, not to be vindictive, that pain is worthwhile. These congregations also need to be willing to accept repentance and offer forgiveness. This is not a matter of ignoring past wrongs or dismissing the idea that reparations may have to be made to overcome those wrongs, but of being willing to forgive the people who have done harm so that all are set free to work toward a just reconciliation together.

Efforts toward reconciliation can lead to improved relationships between groups, but that does not wipe out the pain for many of the people who were harmed by injustice. If we were to use a line graph to demonstrate race relations in the United States, for example, it might show an arrow inching slowly in a positive direction; but that arrow would have many valleys of anger, distrust, and pain along the way. We should not expect the work to be quick or easy. Perhaps the patron saint of this process is the man with the demon-possessed son who cried out honestly to Jesus, "I believe; help my unbelief!" (Mark 9:24).

Chapter Six

Signs of the Times

The mayor scheduled four town meetings over the course of four months. The denominational expert who was leading the meetings maintained a steady hand. She explained that occasional conflict and hurt feelings were not signs that the meetings were failing. Rather, they showed that those in attendance were engaging with each other. Reconciled communities cannot be built without the people in them being honest. This honesty can be hard to hear, and it can hurt others even when we try to share it with tact. Our feelings only get hurt, though, because we are making ourselves vulnerable to what others are saying. That is an important step to reconciliation.

As the people in First Church who attended the meetings heard what the Hispanic participants said, they wondered why the Hispanic perspectives were so new to them. After some thought and discussion, they came to a startlingly obvious conclusion: their congregation had always been white. They never had members who could share alternative views on the town, because they never had members who were from different races or ethnicities. Yes, they had a Hispanic pastor, but she was sent to them, not chosen by them. If they were to help lead the way in a town dealing with its racism, they wondered if they should not be more intentional about seeking diversity in their own membership.

Pursuing greater diversity in their membership made sense, but how could they do it? First Church was over one hundred years old and was in a predominantly white neighborhood. The congregation did have regular contact with the Hispanic neighborhood, but there was no easy public transportation that would carry people between the neighborhood and the church building. Plus, First Church did not want to siphon people away from existing congregations already in the Hispanic neighborhood. As had become their habit, First Church committed to conversation and prayer to seek God's way in this.

This prayer began at the same time First Church was organizing another joint vacation Bible school to be held in the Hispanic neighborhood. The pastor decided to broach the question with the other congregations that were involved. What were they doing about diversity in their memberships?

After several conversations, the pastor found that most of the other congregations were not concerned about diversity.[5] For them, outreach was one thing, and membership was another. You could reach out to all sorts of people, especially poorer people, but it was a one-way activity. The idea of that outreach work circling back to influence the congregation, much less the demographics of the membership, was not on their radar screens.

The one congregation that was open to further conversation was of the same denomination as First Church and was in the Hispanic neighborhood. This was an almost entirely Hispanic congregation that held its worship services in Spanish. First Church had connected with this congregation during its first participation with the joint vacation Bible school, learning much about the neighborhood and becoming acquainted with the neighborhood's leaders through it. The two congregations had also worked closely during the racism meetings.

The First Church pastor visited with the pastor of the Hispanic church. She explained the desire for greater diversity in the First Church congregation and asked if there might be a way the two congregations could work together. The Hispanic pastor empathized, though he made it clear that many of his congregants were not excited about attending a white congregation. They felt marginalized in the larger town, and Sunday morning gave them a chance to feel safe within their own congregation. Yet he felt that First Church had earned enough credibility that some joint activities would be possible.

Both pastors agreed that it would not be wise to force their respective congregations to embrace wide-ranging social interactions with each other immediately. Still, the pastors could lay the groundwork for the people in their congregations to embrace each other more fully. Right now, the people in each congregation tended to

---

5   In a LifeWay research poll, 67 percent of Christians believe their congregation has done enough to be ethnically diverse. Bob Smietana, "Sunday Morning in America Still Segregated—and That's OK with Worshipers," LifeWay Research, January 15, 2015, http://lifewayresearch .com/2015/01/15/sunday-morning-in-america-still-segregated-and-thats-ok-with- worshipers/.

view the other through a pragmatic lens. Each was just a useful partner to the other in vacation Bible school or in racial advocacy. What would happen if the people in each congregation could see the people in the other as members of one common church?

This was not about merging the congregations. Each congregation had its own membership, budget, and governance, and it would stay that way. It was about a change of perspective. So often, congregations view themselves as autonomous little worlds that must be one-stop shops for all the spiritual services people might need. The pastors wanted to break this sort of parochialism, creating a larger picture of what God's church is while also introducing greater diversity to each of their congregations.

By way of baby steps, the pastors decided to have two gatherings: one coordinated by First Church and one hosted by the Hispanic church. First Church would host a large picnic in the summer for both congregations following the vacation Bible school. The people from both congregations would bring their traditional foods to this. The Hispanic congregation would include First Church in their annual celebration of *Las Posadas* (the Lodging), the festival in which people dressed as Mary and Joseph go to different houses in the days leading to Christmas as if they are looking for a place to stay where Mary can give birth. The Hispanic congregation would include houses of First Church members in the visitations by Mary and Joseph. First Pub Church also agreed to be involved by having a second service once a month in a cantina in the Hispanic neighborhood. The Hispanic pastor would coordinate this and work out any language issues. If these initial experiments went well, the pastors would begin planning occasional joint worship services the following year. Minimally, they could swap pulpits once or twice a year now that the new First Church pastor spoke Spanish.

Several months later, as the last night of the *Las Posadas* celebrations was concluding with both First Church and Hispanic church members in attendance, the pastor of the Hispanic church mentioned to the pastor of First Church how amazed he was that there had not been an outbreak of protests and violence earlier in the year. Surprised, the First Church pastor asked what he meant. He explained that following the initial advocacy for the Hispanic community patience in the community began to wear thin. After years of oppression, and the sudden "discovery" of that oppression by town leaders, the Hispanic population was discouraged by how slowly the neighborhood's problems were addressed. Why wouldn't the town start promoting investment in their neighborhood or building pedestrian bridges across the highway or funding their neighborhood schools fully? Why would there be resistance to rectifying these obvious injustices once they had become clear to everyone? Calls within the Hispanic community for protests had begun to surface. The blatant racism on the First Church sign had fueled this. That was until First Church reached out to the neighborhood leaders and asked them to join them in a direct confrontation of the racist attitudes that had led to these problems, providing them a forum to share their frustrations in front of the mayor and the public more broadly. Now, while they understood it might take years to bring the sort of reconciliation that was needed to wipe away the years of injustice, they at least could see real movement in the right direction. This was enough to make them willing to trust the process.

The pastor of First Church shared this with her congregation the following Sunday. The people were shocked. They had no idea there was so much anger. The pastor then pointed to a passage from Luke 12:

> He also said to the crowds, "When you see a cloud rising in the west, you immediately say, 'It is going to rain'; and so it happens. And when you see the south wind blowing, you say, 'There will be scorching heat'; and it happens. You hypocrites! You know how to interpret the appearance of earth and sky, but why do you not know how to interpret the present time? And why do you not judge for yourselves what is right? Thus, when you go with your accuser before a magistrate, on the way make an effort to settle the case, or you may be dragged before the judge, and the judge hand you over to the officer, and the officer throw you in prison. I tell you, you will never get out until you have paid the very last penny." (vv. 54-59)

We so often think we understand a situation, but that understanding comes only from our perspective. It can be easy to miss others' pain when we are comfortable. We want to believe everyone else is comfortable too. If we do not seek to reconcile with those whom we have harmed (or have been complicit in harming because of cultural and social norms), Jesus makes it clear that we will find ourselves facing far worse situations than whatever discomfort comes from working for reconciliation. More than this, by working for reconciliation now, we can be a public witness for God's goodness instead of being humiliated by our accusers when they publicly challenge us because we would not see the need to reconcile with them. We are better disciples, and better able to invite people to become disciples, if we humble ourselves to learn what others see and to work with them based on those perceptions.

The need for reconciling activities may ebb and flow, but having the character of those who are humble and ready to repent and/or forgive is always necessary. Per McNeil, "reconciliation is a dynamic process *and* an objective."[6] To engage in reconciliation as part of the mission of God is for the people in our congregations to allow God to form them in humility all the time. A missional congregation can never settle for a comfortable way of living based on a monocultural or monoracial perspective that is unable to see, identify with, and act to alleviate the pain of others.

Reconciliation ≠ Diversity
While diversity is a desirable outcome of reconciliation, we should not confuse the mission of working for reconciliation with seeking to be diverse. They are not the same thing.

As we have seen, reconciliation is hard work. This is because it is as much about our personal transformation as it is about restoring our relationships with others. It requires growing in the virtues of God, especially humility, and being willing to see ourselves through the eyes of others.

---

6   McNeil, *Roadmap to Reconciliation*, 107.

In contrast, it is easy to become diverse since personal transformation, much less growing in the virtues, is not necessary. Consider how successful vices are at attracting a wide diversity of people. Gambling, sexual promiscuity, alcohol, narcotics, gluttony, hatred, and other vices welcome all comers. Young and old, rich and poor, all races and ethnicities—all are invited with open arms to partake in whatever the vice is. The vices promote diversity but not reconciliation either with God or with each other. While there may be a kind of unity among the people who share in a vice, that unity does not overcome the damaged relationships of the past. It just degrades the humanity of the people who indulge in it, joining them in a common self-destruction.

If we try to force diversity apart from the reconciling mission of God through Jesus Christ, we end up with an idol. Jesus becomes no more than a mascot who cheers our diversity. He has nothing else to say to us about how to pattern our lives, much less about becoming his disciples. He just wants us all to be together regardless of how we live or worship. This is an obvious failure of mission! The Great Commission not only tells us to go to "all nations" but also to make "disciples of all nations" (Matt 28:19). The coming of the Holy Spirit at Pentecost then made it possible for us to live in reconciled ways with one another as disciples of Jesus Christ.

Diversity was never meant to be the chief end of our mission. Rather, it is a gift that God gives us to demonstrate we are being faithful in our mission. Psalm 133 makes this point:

> How very good and pleasant it is when kindred live together in unity! It is like the precious oil on the head, running down upon the beard, on the beard of Aaron, running down over the collar of his robes. It is like the dew of Hermon, which falls on the mountains of Zion. For there the LORD ordained his blessing, life forevermore.

Aaron was already a faithful servant of God. The oil of consecration was an outward demonstration of God's blessing on him. Likewise, Zion refers to the holy city of Jerusalem where God promised to be. Mount Hermon is a high, well-watered mountain in Israel. To have the dew from Hermon come to the more arid area of Zion would be a sign of God's pleasure with the already sanctified city. So it is with diversity. When we have committed ourselves to be faithful to the Great Commission, inviting others to be reconciled first to God through Jesus Christ and then to each other in the love of Christ, God brings the blessing of diversity in our congregations. That a diverse congregation can live in unity together as a reconciled community becomes a sign to others of God's presence with us.

Reconciliation does not just promote diversity but unity among diverse peoples. It is this unity in diversity that those outside the church can find so impressive, as seen in how the people in Antioch responded to the church there.

By practicing reconciliation, we avoid short-circuiting our mission by focusing on diversity. We can then celebrate the diversity that God gives us as we work toward reconciliation that is centered around the common reconciliation God offers to all through Christ.

When we have received this blessing of being part of a diverse community that is reconciled to God and one another, it does not mean we can leave reconciliation behind as an item we have checked off our to-do list. McNeil suggests that once we have committed to live in relationship with people who are different from us, there are tactics we can use to continue in the mission of God through reconciliation. These are

- Information gathering: constantly learning about the situation surrounding us and how others view it;
- Reflective thinking: synthesizing other people's perspectives with our thinking, even allowing our thinking to be modified by it;
- Strategic storytelling: learning to tell our stories even as we hear others' stories. No matter our background, our story, especially how we have experienced God's work in our lives, is valuable and needs to be heard in a reconciled community;
- Community building: staying in relationship with

different people and continuing to invite new people into those relationships by creating safe spaces for them to share their stories and hear our stories;

- Intercultural communication: developing the skills to understand the values and assumptions underneath people's stories;
- Inductive learning skills: being able to understand people by observation, learning their meaning from how they act in addition to the content of their words;
- Conflict resolution: knowing that conflict is a natural part of living into a reconciled community, be ready to deal with conflict in a healthy way rather than in a way that ignores it or that forces one group's power over another's;
- Problem solving: working together as a reconciled community to deal with external situations of injustice as they present themselves, so our congregations can be a public witness to the reconciling love of God.[7]

Prior to the full establishment of the kingdom of God, the world will need to see examples of how God's salvation includes creating a reconciled community. Our congregations have the unique opportunity to bear a public witness of what God's kingdom is like through taking on the missionary work of reconciliation. As we succeed in this, we will have a powerful reason for people to accept our invitation to become disciples of Jesus Christ, and we will have healthy communities in which they can be nurtured as disciples.

Key Tactics: How We Can Work for Reconciliation

- Study the nature of God's work to reconcile humanity through Jesus Christ.
- For privileged congregations: recognize your privilege and adopt a quiet, listening attitude to hear and acknowledge the pain others feel.
- For non-privileged congregations: speak up so that

---

7   Ibid., 111–13.

those who are privileged can understand your pain and the ways they have, perhaps unknowingly, contributed to it. Be prepared to forgive without abandoning calls for rectifying unjust situations.

- Learn to tell your entire experience of relating to God. Don't just focus on getting to the happy ending of glory, but acknowledge the struggles you have had with God along the way. This can help you to be more understanding of listening to others who are working through their difficulties in relating to other groups while trying to reconcile with them.
- Be willing to ask for help. This is a difficult and painful process. Contact people you trust to help you move through it.
- Invite everyone who is part of the broken relationship to the discussion. You cannot reconcile if you do not have the other parties participating.
- Use the relationships you have to create appropriate space for the conversations about reconciliation, especially if you are working in the larger community. You may want to talk to the local police force, political leaders, and others.
- Remember that discomfort during the process of reconciliation is not a sign of failure. It can be a sign that people are taking seriously what they hear from each other and are going through the transformation of seeing themselves and the world differently.
- Seek congregational diversity by looking beyond the congregation. Help people recognize they are part of the full church of Christ along with other Christians in other congregations. Building relationships with sister churches that connect in missional and social ways is helpful for this.
- Include sister church events in your announcements— not as a special advertisement or announcement, but as a regular announcement.

- If you engage with a reconciliation issue, whether in your congregation or the larger community, remember that it takes time to change people. Brenda Salter Mc-Neil's steps discussed earlier (page 103) are helpful to move through this change: realization of the problem, identification of the groups with each other, preparation to make a change, and activation of that change.
- Follow the steps laid out by McNeil for staying in the process of reconciliation (page 112–13).

CHAPTER SEVEN

IT'S OK TO PARTY!

Deuteronomy 32:49
Ecclesiastes 9:7-10; Isaiah 55:12

In the movie *Footloose*, John Lithgow plays Shaw Moore, a pastor who spearheaded making rock music and dancing illegal in the small town where he serves. When Ren McCormack, played by Kevin Bacon, moves into the town, he challenges this restriction and leads the local teenagers—including Reverend Moore's daughter—in an effort to overturn the pastor's position by having a high school prom.

Well into the movie, we find out that Reverend Moore is not inherently against dancing. Rather, he is frightened that the town's teenagers might find themselves in danger if he allows a dance. It is revealed that he had an older son who was killed in a car accident when driving to a dance, and he does not want to put his daughter, or anyone else's children, in harm's way. In the end, Reverend Moore relents, the law is repealed, and the prom is held.

A pivotal scene that explains why Reverend Moore begins rethinking his position occurs about halfway through the movie when Ren comes before the town council to argue in favor of dancing. Far from a teenage rant against unfair laws, Ren uses the Bible as his primary support. He points to King David and the psalmists as examples of those who danced to celebrate. He also quotes Ecclesiastes, saying there is "a time to dance." Rather than the Bible being a

117

mournful, stern, or unfeeling book, he explains that it makes room for joy. The Bible recognizes that life is a gift worth celebrating, and it prompts people to demonstrate that. Sometimes we are supposed to party!

Congregations are not known for throwing the best parties. We have our pie auctions, fall festivals, trunk-or-treats, Christmas celebrations, Easter breakfasts, and potluck suppers, but we rarely have full-on parties. Maybe when one of the people in our congregations gets married we have a party at the reception, but that is not really a congregational party. It is a party where people from the congregation happen to be present. Perhaps, like Reverend Moore, that is because many of us are uncomfortable mixing our enjoyment of life too much with our faith. We may fear that the one will contaminate the other.

Certainly, being missional seems to require setting aside celebrations. All the discipline and sacrifice we need to address the pains and struggles of the world make parties seem superfluous. The Bible may speak of a time for dancing, but it appears that time is not now. Now we have the hard work of making disciples to occupy our time.

Jesus would seem to exemplify this. The Bible never describes him as smiling or laughing. Yes, he attended at least one wedding party and some feasts, but we never see him enjoying them. Hebrews 12:2 suggests that Jesus endured the cross because he saw joy in the future, but he is never depicted as being joyful during his earthly ministry.

G. K. Chesterton, a well-known late nineteenth/early twentieth-century Christian apologist in Britain, indicated that the reason the Bible does not talk about Jesus being joyful might be different from what we think. Perhaps, wrote Chesterton, Jesus was so full of joy, and that joy was so potent, that he needed to shield us from seeing it. He went on to explain:

> Joy, which was the small publicity of the pagan, is the gigantic secret of the Christian. And as I close this chaotic volume I open again the strange small book from which all Christianity came; and I am again haunted by a kind of confirmation. The tremendous figure which fills the Gospels towers

in this respect, as in every other, above all the thinkers who ever thought themselves tall. His pathos was natural, almost casual. The Stoics, ancient and modern, were proud of concealing their tears. He never concealed His tears; He showed them plainly on His open face at any daily sight, such as the far sight of His native city. Yet He concealed something. Solemn supermen and imperial diplomatists are proud of restraining their anger. He never restrained His anger. He flung furniture down the front steps of the Temple, and asked men how they expected to escape the damnation of Hell. Yet He restrained something. I say it with reverence; there was in that shattering personality a thread that must be called shyness. There was something that He hid from all men when He went up a mountain to pray. There was something that He covered constantly by abrupt silence or impetuous isolation. There was some one thing that was too great for God to show us when He walked upon our earth; and I have sometimes fancied that it was His mirth.[1]

Whether we accept Chesterton's argument or not, it is fair to say that the Gospels preclude us from believing that Jesus did enjoy himself at times. They tell us that Jesus attended parties and even got slandered as "a glutton and a drunkard, a friend of tax collectors and sinners" (Matt 11:19; Luke 7:34). He also turned water into wine at the wedding feast in Cana "after the guests [had] become drunk" (John 2:10). This at least hints that he was not averse to enjoying himself and that he was not against other people enjoying themselves.

Of course, joy is not the same as enjoying oneself. Joy is a virtue that the Holy Spirit develops in us as we learn to take pleasure in what pleases God. Enjoying ourselves is a brief experience of fun. It is possible to be joyful when we are not having fun and to have fun without being formed in the virtue of joy. Most of us have experienced this!

---

1   G. K. Chesterton, *Orthodoxy* (New York: John Lane Co., 1908), 298–99.

Still, the two are not completely disconnected. After all, if we are filled with joy by the Spirit, shouldn't that joy at least sometimes be visible in how we enjoy the world around us? Likewise, if we enjoy ourselves in a specific moment, is that not a means by which the Spirit beckons us to be filled more fully with God's joy? And, what could give us more reason to enjoy ourselves and be filled with joy than seeing God work as we participate in God's mission?

There are multiple places in the Bible that link joy to the mission of God, even showing people involved in God's mission enjoying themselves. The first two parables in Luke 15 are an example of this. After a shepherd finds his lost sheep, and a widow finds her lost coin, both call their friends and neighbors to rejoice. The successful completion of a mission is reason to throw a party. In addition to these parties on earth, Jesus follows up each story by saying that when a sinner repents "there will be more joy in heaven" (v. 7) and there will be "joy in the presence of the angels of God" (v. 10). In other words, God is joyful when even small portions of God's mission are accomplished.

Paul likewise exulted when he saw successful outcomes from his evangelistic work. In 1 Thessalonians 2:19-20, he states that he has profound joy because of those who accepted the gospel under his ministry: "For what is our hope or joy or crown of boasting before our Lord Jesus at his coming? Is it not you? Yes, you are our glory and joy!"

The saints and angels in heaven also celebrate when God's mission is successful. Revelation 19 shows them burst into song after God conquers Babylon, ending an ancient evil that had seduced people away from God's grace for millennia.

But not all rejoicing needs to wait for part of God's mission to be completed. The final parable in Luke 15, often called the parable of the prodigal son, suggests this.

In the story, the younger son demands his inheritance early and leaves home to live immorally. The older son stays home to work in his father's fields. When the first son returns and repents, the father throws a lavish celebration. While this looks like the same sort of celebration that occurs after God's redemptive mission is completed, we find out that the celebration never had to wait. We learn this from a conversation the father has with his older son.

Disgusted by his father's extravagant party on behalf of his younger brother, the older son refuses to celebrate. When the father comes to him, the older son explains that the father never threw a party for him even though he had been faithful for years. The father responds with a startling revelation: "Son, you are always with me, and all that is mine is yours" (v. 31). In saying this, the father points out that he had always been ready to celebrate with his son. The father's wealth was always ready for the son to enjoy. It is just that the older son never asked to celebrate with the father.

The problem was that both boys thought they could only experience joy once their time working for their father was done. The younger son rebelled against this and acted as if the father were dead, taking his inheritance and squandering it on cheap thrills that only imitate joy in a hollow way. The older son resigned himself to being a slave, telling himself his father would be dead soon enough. Then he would inherit everything and celebrate. Both sons wanted their father dead because both thought their father stood in the way of joy. In fact, the father was desperate to be the source of joy for his children. The father was always ready to live out his joy with his boys. They just never understood it.

This is often our congregations' failure. Like the younger son, we may feel that we must break away from the moral teachings of the Bible so we have license to support the way people in the culture want to pursue cheap thrills. Or, like the older son, we become severe, rejecting the idea of enjoying ourselves as frivolous and worthy of condemnation until we have some major accomplishment worth celebrating.

Given that our congregations tend to exhibit one of these two traits, it is little wonder we struggle to have people join us. We become unnecessary, either giving people permission for something they already feel free to do, or telling people they must defer experiencing joy until God accomplishes something great. Either way, we fail in Christ's commission to make disciples. Both kill joy because both ignore that God desires to be a fountain of joy for us now, *while* we are engaged in God's mission. Just as God allows us to participate in the fullness of God's mission, God shares the fullness of God's joy with us so we can enjoy life even as we commit ourselves to the hard work of mission. In doing this, we can let go of thinking joy is only found through moral license or through waiting for a great event to happen.

The God whose mission we are joining is a joyful God who desires us to be as joyful as those who are saved by God's grace and engaged in God's mission. To be missional, our congregations should be hubs of that joy, bathing everything we do with it. This joy flows naturally from God to us. We just need to claim it and share it.

The Mountaintop

The pastor and some members from First Church were on their way home from a conference on multiethnic ministries. The conference had been inspiring, including excellent worship, great music, and encouraging speakers. One of the lay leaders made a comment often repeated by church people when returning from a good conference: "I wish we could bottle this feeling and keep it with us all the time! It always seems a shame that we have to lose this mountaintop experience when we get back."

This got the others thinking. Why not find a way to help the rest of the people at First Church enjoy the mountaintop? While they couldn't recreate the conference, there were reasons for the congregation to celebrate. They didn't have to bring in outside enthusiasm; they could acknowledge and celebrate what God already had done in their midst.

It had been nearly two years since First Church had welcomed their new pastor. Much had happened during that time. The congregation had experienced all the regular bumps and scrapes in a pastoral transition. However, they kept these in perspective and moved through them without any lasting discontent or broken relationships. They had lost the one group of people, but most of the congregation had stood firm. They had even attracted a few new members, including some young families who previously had kept their distance after the scandal with the music director.

The town racism meetings had concluded with the mayor creating a permanent task force for the Hispanic neighborhood leaders to engage with the town council. First Church's pastor and the pastor from the Hispanic church were both asked to serve on the task force.

The joint endeavors by First Church and the Hispanic church had flourished on all fronts. The First Church members loved being part of *Las Posadas* and had thrown a grand picnic in the Hispanic neighborhood following a record number of children participating in the vacation Bible school held in the park. A pulpit exchange between the churches had also gone well and paved the road for joint worship services.

First Pub Church was going strong and had even planted First Cantina Church as a congregation. After meeting in both the pub and the cantina for several months, and attracting a growing number of people from the Hispanic neighborhood, they decided that it would be good for a group of people to meet regularly in the cantina while the pub folks stayed in their original venue. First Cantina Church was jointly sponsored by First Church and the Hispanic church and used Spanish in its gatherings.

In all of these things, new disciples of Jesus Christ were being made. Whether the new members at First Church, the Hispanic church, First Pub Church, or First Cantina Church, it was clear people were coming to Jesus and committing to live by his teachings. Likewise, the broader witness of these congregations had created a better atmosphere in the town overall.

There was much to celebrate! The leaders talked about how they could set up a congregational party where they could give thanks for all the good missional work God had done through them. At the party, they would let people from all the related congregations share their personal experiences of participating in the mission. They would also record brief videos of people's stories about God's work and show those on the Sunday mornings leading up to the party. But that led to another question.

The leaders did not just want the people in the congregations to see these missional successes as one-off reasons to celebrate. They wanted to enjoy God's presence and power with them all the time, even during the hard or tedious times of being in mission. Missional work should be doorways through which the congregations experienced God's joy in an ongoing way. After all, it gave them front-row seats to the supernatural work of God's kingdom bursting forth into the town.

The leaders wanted the party to send the right message: Look at the good God has done through us. Let's celebrate it! Look at the missional work God is allowing us to continue doing in the name of Jesus Christ. Let's celebrate as we do the work.

That was the trick. Like many good Protestant congregations, the people of First Church would acknowledge good things or accomplishments when they reported on the "old business" at their various committees, but they would quickly shift their focus to the "new business." There was barely a chance to catch one's breath, much less celebrate. There was even less of an opportunity to share in the joyful presence of God while doing missional work. How could the leaders help break through this?

> On that very day the LORD addressed Moses as follows: "Ascend this mountain of the Abarim, Mount Nebo, which is in the land of Moab, across from Jericho, and view the land of Canaan, which I am giving to the Israelites for a possession; you shall die there on the mountain that you ascend and shall be gathered to your kin, as your brother Aaron died on Mount Hor and was gathered to his kin; because both of you broke faith with me among the Israelites at the waters of Meribath-kadesh in the wilderness of Zin, by failing to maintain my holiness among the Israelites. Although you may view the land from a distance, you shall not enter it— the land that I am giving to the Israelites." (Deut 32:48-52)

In this passage, God tells Moses to climb Mount Nebo to view the Promised Land. God explains that Moses will die on the mountain, barred from entering the Promised Land because of his sins. God would allow Moses to survey what God would accomplish for the people of Israel, but Moses could not participate in the completion of that mission. The people of Israel still would have much to do after Moses died. As grim as this passage is, with its talk of death and punishment for sin, God is offering Moses a chance to experience joy. God gives Moses the assurance that Israel's mission will continue until it reaches its glorious end. That is reason to celebrate. Even though his part in the mission is over, Moses can savor the joy of knowing God will be faithful as Israel continues to participate in God's mission.

There are three reasons conventional wisdom gives us to explain why God was wrong to give Moses an opportunity to celebrate.

First, we cheapen joy if we celebrate at the wrong time. We are warned not to count our chickens before they hatch, lest we end up looking foolish for claiming success before we have clinched it. By this logic, God should not allow Moses to rejoice by seeing the Promised Land. There was too much work left to do! The mission was far from complete.

Second, work is not a source of joy. The way we organize our lives, separating "work" from "leisure," "weekdays" from "weekends," and "effort" from "relaxation," tells us that we should not mix work and joy. Work is a drudgery we must endure. We can only enjoy life when we stop working. Again, by this logic God should not only forbid Moses to celebrate, but forbid any experience of joy, because the Israelites still had so much work left to do.

Third, Moses failed. He had sinned, causing God's punishment to fall on him and causing Israel to be deprived of their greatest leader. This failure is the final stroke. God may have done great things through Moses, but the fact that Moses left the Israelites with so much incomplete work because of his failure means that God should demand that he die in repentance and sorrow rather than joy.

Yet God's wisdom is not our wisdom (paraphrased from Isa 55:8-9). We assume that it is up to each of us, or our congregations, to complete all of God's mission. That is wrong. The completion of God's mission is not dependent on human effort. It is dependent on God, and God will not fail. For this reason, we can celebrate even when we have a long way to go in the mission. We celebrate because we trust God will accomplish what God has set out to do.

125

We celebrate that as sinful and faulty as we are, we are part of this mission, knowing that God will redeem even our failures and set all things right.

It is based on this wisdom—that God works through us to accomplish God's purposes even when we cannot or will not—that we can do more than celebrate. We can be formed in joy. Joy is not a feeling we earn; it is a virtue, a gift of the Holy Spirit. It is a character trait of God that the Holy Spirit generates and nurtures in us, like love, peace, patience, goodness, faithfulness, or kindness. Joy is taking pleasure in God and God's handiwork no matter what our circumstances are. God's faithfulness to carry out God's mission gives us a solid reason for being joyful.

One way we can grow in the virtue of joy is to celebrate whenever we see God's faithfulness. And, since God is always faithful, there are always reasons for celebration! It may be that a congregational program has reached a milestone, even if a minor one. It may be that one of the individuals in the congregation has experienced God's presence in a special way. It may be that there is some act of God in the neighborhood, town, city, county, nation, or world that we have seen. Whatever it is, if it demonstrates God is at work to accomplish God's purposes, we can celebrate it. We can take joy in what God has done, is doing, and will do.

Giving thanks is a primary way congregations can celebrate. They can make time in their worship or other gatherings for people to give their testimonies about God's goodness to them. They can include times of thanks in their corporate prayer instead of just focusing on petitions. Church reports should explicitly offer thanks and invite people in the committee to celebrate as they describe what has happened in the congregation.

Congregations can even have parties, dinners, or other special events to celebrate God's faithfulness. These should not be forced social events that become one more item that members feel obliged to attend, but should arise whenever they seem appropriate as a spiritual discipline of celebration. They should be real celebrations in which we give thanks to God for the good God has done, is doing, and will do. God is worthy of our celebrations!

We have prayer lines and ministries where we are quick to share our struggles and sadness, yet we often withhold our reasons for happiness for fear of coming across as boastful about the good things God has done in our lives. Yet joy boasts only in God. If God has been faithful, we need to take every opportunity to give God credit for this and to rejoice together. Doing this is no different from how Jesus described the celebrations of the shepherd who found his sheep, the woman who found her coin, and the father whose son returned. People who knew God's goodness in their own lives called everyone together to celebrate it!

Joy is God's gift to us, and if we practice it by celebrating God's faithfulness whenever we can, even when we are knee-deep in difficult missional work, we enhance our participation in God's mission. We are engaging in mission by whatever work we are doing, but also by growing into the character of God through accepting the gift of joy and by witnessing to those around us that God is active in this world for our good. Our joy is not limited to moments of success but is unbounded because we can see our God's goodness even in difficult times. Being a disciple of such a joyful God is a wonderful thing!

L'Chaim — To Life!

> Go, eat your bread with enjoyment, and drink your wine with a merry heart; for God has long ago approved what you do. Let your garments always be white; do not let oil be lacking on your head. Enjoy life with the wife whom you love, all the days of your vain life that are given you under the sun, because that is your portion in life and in your toil at which you toil under the sun. Whatever your hand finds to do, do with your might; for there is no work or thought or knowledge or wisdom in Sheol, to which you are going. (Eccl 9:7-10)

In the passage from Deuteronomy, there is a clear connection between joy and mission. Moses is a participant in God's mission to bring the people of Israel into the Promised Land. While Moses will not be part of completing that mission, he can share God's joy by celebrating God's faithfulness to continue working with Israel.

The passage from Ecclesiastes is different. There is no story of God's mission here. There is just the command to enjoy life in the face of certain death.

Ecclesiastes is one of the darkest books of the Bible. It begins and ends with the proclamation that everything is meaningless. Life is full of difficulties and tragedies that no one can foresee or stop. No matter how hard we work, how well we live, or how much we learn, we are still subject to the vicissitudes of daily life. Ecclesiastes 9:11 makes this point: "I saw that under the sun the race is not to the swift, nor the battle to the strong, nor bread to the wise, nor riches to the intelligent, nor favor to the skillful; but time and chance happen to them all."

This is a grim assessment. Any given moment is pregnant with possible disaster. The best we can hope for is a safe passage through life. Even if we are granted this, we still end up dead. This is hardly a missional way of thinking!

What message can Ecclesiastes provide us about being in mission given this dark view? At best, it might tell us to hunker down and minimize our exposure to danger, which runs counter to the missional work of making disciples. At worst, it might tell us we should become joy-killers, convincing people that nothing matters. We could tell them it is the height of stupidity to celebrate anything. Such joy is ignorant of the capricious reality we live in and the impending grave that stands open to swallow us.

Sadly, Christians have often adopted this sort of joy-killing as our mission. We do this by focusing only on eternity. We call people to disdain both the troubles and pleasures of life as fruitless distractions. They should renounce these things as unimportant compared to the eternal existence God has for us.

That may sound pious, compelling people to give up their physical attachments to gain a better eternity, but it is far less than what God gives us in Jesus Christ. God never intended the physical world to stand in contrast to the eternal world. God created all of it and called it good. Likewise, Jesus was both fully human and fully divine. The joy God has for us eternally is the same joy God desires us to be formed by now.

Jesus said, "The thief comes only to steal and kill and destroy. I came that they may have life, and have it abundantly" (John 10:10). To steal or kill others' joy is to be aligned not with Jesus but with the devil! It is also to miss the abundance of what God offers in Christ. Abundant life does not just start once our bodies fall away in death. It starts today! To miss the joy available in the enjoyments of this physical life is to diminish the joy we will experience eternally.

This is the logic of Ecclesiastes. During all the uncertainties of life, and the looming reality of death, the author commends us to enjoy our lives here and now. This advice even has a missional ring to it. As with the Great Commission, we are told to "go." As we go, we are to eat, drink, enjoy our wives (or husbands—a reference to sex among the other enjoyments of marriage), and to put our hearts into doing whatever is set before us.

This enjoyment is not a license for us to do whatever makes us feel good. The last two verses of Ecclesiastes tell us "Fear God, and keep his commandments; for that is the whole duty of everyone. For God will bring every deed into judgment, including every secret thing, whether good or evil" (Eccl 12:13-14). The author assures us that how we live matters, since God will judge our lives. This does not mean that we must forego the pleasures of our physical life, just that we enjoy them within our call to make disciples.

Strange as it may sound to us, enjoying life is essential to being effective in Christ's Great Commission. If we are people who can demonstrate the joy of God by enjoying the physical pleasures of life—eating, drinking, sex, and so on—we will be more attractive to the people in the world around us as we invite them into discipleship.

We may want to push back at this point. Aren't there dangers in linking the enjoyment of physical pleasures to the Great Commission? Physical pleasures lead so easily to sin. Isn't eating too much the sin of gluttony? Isn't drinking too much alcohol the sin of drunkenness? Isn't indulging in sex the pathway to lust? Even if we don't sin by indulging in physical pleasures, won't they at least be a distraction from calling people to be disciples of Jesus Christ? Won't our participation in God's mission suffer if we are constantly pausing to enjoy ourselves? Jesus is consistent about saying we need to sacrifice to be his disciples. Based on that, much of the Christian mission historically has included teaching people to restrain their physical desires.

These are understandable concerns, especially because there is so much cultural controversy and confusion around physical pleasure. We do need to tread carefully in addressing them.

There is nothing wrong with enjoying ourselves physically. It would seem strange for God to have created us to enjoy delicious foods and drinks or to feel good when we have sex if God only intended us to feel guilty when we did these things. God created our bodies with the ability to experience physical pleasure because God wants us to enjoy God's good creation.

However, much like disciple-making in the Great Commission, that enjoyment is to happen as we go about our lives, and our lives are to be focused on making disciples. We are meant to enjoy physical pleasures as we make disciples in our daily lives; we are not to seek those pleasures in place of making disciples.

As we are formed into God's joy by enjoying these various pleasures, we demonstrate a winsome and attractive example of what a disciple of Jesus Christ looks like. People see that being a disciple is not about being a prude but about being someone who can enjoy life even when we know that tragedy and death are real.

The problem comes not when we enjoy physical things but when we make physical enjoyment our purpose in life. This not only keeps us from participating in God's mission but devalues our humanity. We reduce ourselves to following our physical instincts. If we proceed down this path for too long, we become self-destructive, controlled by those instincts. Addicts, people who make the pursuit of pleasure their life's mission, whether by choice or because of a sickness, are a sad example of this.

God, however, allows us to enjoy the physical pleasures of life without making pleasure our mission. Far from pulling us away from God into a lifestyle of dissipation, they draw us closer to God as we come to recognize that God gives us these pleasures as good gifts. James 1:17 explains, "Every perfect gift, is from above, coming down from the Father of lights." Psalm 104:14-15 tells us that these gifts include those things that give us physical pleasure: "You cause the grass to grow for the cattle, and plants for people to use, to bring forth food from the earth, and wine to gladden the human heart, oil to make the face shine, and bread to strengthen the human heart."

It is true that these good gifts can be perverted, but that is true of any good gift God has given us. Food, wine, and sex can be used immorally, but so can theology, worship, and singing. The issue is not whether it is possible for something to be perverted; the issue is whether something can be brought into the service of God's mission. If it can be, we should embrace it!

If we reject physical pleasure, we diminish our capacity to engage in God's mission in two ways. First, we reduce our ability to relate to God, who is the source of the good things we can enjoy. Second, it becomes harder for us to relate to people, since so many people are seeking after physical pleasures in their daily lives.

The same holds true for congregations. If our congregations cannot appreciate these pleasures and guide people in how to receive them as disciples of Jesus Christ, we will become less capable of relating to God and people. Our worship will become more arid, and our conversation with people will seem unnaturally rigid because we will always be guarding against the danger of enjoying life too much. We will probably seem like incomplete human beings to those outside the church. That's because we will have cut ourselves off from some of what God intended humans to enjoy.

Sadly, this is exactly how many of our congregations are viewed already. People see congregations as groups where normal life, especially enjoying physical pleasures, is either badly misunderstood or condemned. This causes people outside the church to shut down from wanting to hear about Jesus. They have judged our congregations before listening to our message because they believe our congregations have already judged them for enjoying physical pleasures.

This disconnect is not only with people outside the church. Even those of us within the church often keep walls up between us because we are uncomfortable about broaching these issues with each other. If we are honest, many of us live in a space between prudish Christianity and enjoyment of physical pleasures. This can lead us either to having a perpetually guilty conscience, because we think our enjoyment is always sinful, or to compartmentalizing our faith away from our daily lives. Either way, when in Christian company, we refuse to acknowledge the physical pleasures we enjoy. This might ease our consciences a bit. We can claim to be a Christian, since we devote some of our public time and effort to our faith, and we can enjoy our physical pleasures when we are safely out of the church's view.

What a difference it would make if we could tear down this wall of separation. Imagine if our congregations were places where people could acknowledge enjoying the physical pleasures of life, giving praise to God as the source of those pleasures. Our congregations would be places where we could come to enjoy good meals, where we could trust sex would be discussed in open and healthy ways, and where God would be depicted as wanting people to enjoy the good things in life.

If we practiced joy this way, we would be doing mission. People outside the church would see Christians as the most joyful group of people. That joy would be evident because Christians would unashamedly enjoy physical pleasures during their daily lives. From this, we would have the credibility to offer a constructive way of approaching the pleasures of life rather than the stilted moralism we so often retreat to because of our hang-ups around physical pleasure.

None of this is to say that we must start drinking alcohol, eating fine foods, or having more sex with our spouses if we are to be missional. We can be missional even if we abstain from certain foods, drinks, sex, or other pleasures. In fact, sometimes mission demands we forego these pleasures to demonstrate a better way of living. The issue is not what we do or don't do; the issue is whether we are demonstrating joy. Too often when we abstain from physical pleasures, we do it in a way that is judgmental toward those who do partake in them. We are called to demonstrate as much joy in our abstention as in our partaking (Matt 6:16-18). Either way, we can celebrate God as the Giver of good things.

In a world that only understands indulgence or prohibition, the ability to be formed in joy by enjoying the pleasures God gives us is profoundly missional. Most people know that the pursuit of physical pleasure alone leads to emptiness, but they don't know what to do about it. They sometimes feel they must swing between indulgence on the weekends and relative seriousness on the weekdays, between what they do for fun and what they do to survive. We can offer so much more to the people around us, demonstrating joy that allows people to celebrate the physical pleasures in their daily lives in a way that fulfills their humanity and honors God.

How can we practice this sort of pleasure-affirming, missional joy in our congregations? Hospitality is an important first step. By hospitality, I do not mean the brief period after worship when snacks are served. I mean a much deeper practice in which we share the gifts God has given us in a mutual way.

We first practice hospitality among those who are already part of the congregation. This requires us to have a greater vulnerability with each other, overcoming the shame many of us have learned toward physical pleasures. We often do not discuss the things that bring us physical pleasure, because we feel they are not appropriate in church. We need to move past this.

I am not suggesting that we start discussing our sexual activities or sharing about our favorite drinks when we gather for worship. I am suggesting that we can be more open about our entire lives with each other. This includes sharing about what physical things we enjoy and helping each other see how God is the Giver of all these things.

As we learn to discuss these pleasures with each other, we can show hospitality to those outside the congregation. We do this by sharing the best we have: the best food, the best experience of worship, the best music, and the best of everything else. We do this so they can experience some pleasure and so we can call them to become disciples of a God who wants them to be joyful.

When we make it clear that we are comfortable dealing with physical pleasure, those who are not disciples of Jesus Christ will know they can bring their whole selves to church, even the parts they may have thought Christians frowned upon. We will need to help them recognize that those pleasures are gifts from God, but they will be ready to hear that from us. The fact that we are open about how we enjoy physical pleasures will make us trustworthy to speak about these things.

A congregation's hospitality should not just be extended to those who are seeking for pleasure in their daily lives but to those who have been broken by indulging in those pleasures. Making space for alcoholics, drug users, sex addicts, overeaters, and others who need to recover from addiction is an act of mission. These people should not be treated with disdain but welcomed as they search for joy. Even our broken desires for pleasure are whispers of our longing for God and the joy God gives.[2]

First Church found God's joy in hosting an enormous party that included the Hispanic church, First Pub Church, and First Cantina Church. Each group brought their own food, and each brought their own stories about how they had seen and felt God's goodness over the past two years. The younger folks even put together a video montage of the congregations' activities over the years, which was in both Spanish and English. The highlight was a piñata that the children from the various congregations all had fun breaking! The members of each congregation enjoyed the wonderful cooking and diversities of food the others brought to the table. They truly had begun to feel like they were one big church. Following the party, several other potlucks and similar dinners were scheduled to continue the sense of community, with the Hispanic church and First Church alternating as hosts.

First Pub Church and First Cantina Church had another item they wanted to address. Over the past two years, they had become convicted about the alcoholism they witnessed in their respective locations. These congregations had been planted in part because the

---

2   C. S. Lewis discusses how even the most immoral human desires are indicative of the human longing to find spiritual peace. He suggests that God can purify those desires so that they draw the person to God instead of away from God. C. S. Lewis, *The Great Divorce* (New York: Macmillan, 1946), 69–70, 98–105.

people who attended them wanted to continue to gather in a way that allowed them to enjoy their favorite drinks as they worshiped God. However, the members of both congregations began to recognize many of the people who came to the pub and the cantina at the same time they did every week. The members saw how these people were getting worn down physically by alcohol. In building relationships with them, the congregation members learned about the impact of drinking on relationships and jobs.

The members of FPC and FCC approached the pastors of First Church and the Hispanic church about creating recovery groups that people in the pub and cantina could attend. The pastors got in touch with organizations such as Celebrate Recovery and Alcoholics Anonymous to look at possible options. They also spoke to the local courthouse to see what needs there were for recovery groups in the area. Based on this, the pastors agreed to host recovery groups in the congregations' respective buildings, one for English speakers and one for Spanish speakers.

The recovery groups filled almost immediately, including people from the congregations. Some participants in the groups were members who had attended for years, but no one had realized they were alcoholics. One of these members told the First Church pastor that he had fought this demon in silence for a long time. By opening the conversation, the congregation had helped him to find genuine joy because he didn't have to hide his challenges any longer.

Hope and Joy

As the leaders from First Church watched their ways of promoting God's joy take shape in the congregations, they continued to think about what had blessed them during the conference on multiethnic ministries that had prompted the joint celebration with the Hispanic congregation and the pub and cantina churches. Several of them remembered a specific worship leader. She was an African American who had spoken eloquently about the difficulties that she, her family, and her congregation faced because of racism in the United States. After reciting these injustices, she burst into the gospel song "By and By, When the Morning Comes." Stirred by her spirited singing, the audience joined in the chorus "By and by, when the morning comes, when all the saints of God are gathered home, we will tell the story how we've overcome. We will understand it better by and by."

As the leaders from First Church reflected on what made this moment so powerful for them, they shared about how joy and hope intersected in that moment. It was not that the worship leader was unaware of or downplaying the problems she faced. It was that she could look at those struggles and still have hope that God would set all things right in the end. Trusting that, she was filled with joy and could praise God. She claimed God's victory not only over the evils she faced but over all evil.

> For you shall go out in joy, and be led back in peace; the mountains and the hills before you shall burst into song, and all the trees of the field shall clap their hands. Instead of the thorn shall come up the cypress; instead of the brier shall come up the myrtle; and it shall be to the LORD for a memorial, for an everlasting sign that shall not be cut off. (Isa 55:12-13)

The last chapters of Isaiah are focused on God's ultimate victory. Written in uncertain and dangerous times for the people of Israel, these passages prompted God's people to look beyond the moment in which they lived to a day when all creation would be renewed and joy would flow unchecked. Even the trees and hills would explode in delight before God, and the people of God would go out in joy to join their celebration. Hope gives us reason for joy.

There is much in the world that tries to keep God's joy from filling us. War, famine, child abuse, sex trafficking, broken families, violence, poverty, hatred, and death are just some of the painful realities that make joy seem impossible or foolish. However, when we have hope, we can acknowledge the depth of this pain and still be joyful. Hope is the gift of the Holy Spirit to see God setting all things right even as we acknowledge how grim things are today. When we accept this gift of hope, we are freed to take pleasure in the good gifts of God even though there are many tragedies around us.

Being formed by hope so that we can also be formed by joy is missional. Where joy opens the door for us to relate to people in their pursuit of physical pleasure, hope allows us to relate to people during profound sorrow and inexplicable horror. It is the gift God gives us so that we have an answer after the latest mass shooting, terror attack, or personal loss. That answer is not to explain why something happened but to provide a firm assurance that the evil we witnessed and pain we felt is not the final word because God's mission to redeem all things through Jesus Christ has not been overturned. That assurance is so strong that we can even lift our voices to praise God in the midst of the pain.

Being formed by the Holy Spirit in hope is an essential part of our mission. If Christians can be hopeful when terrible tragedies occur, we are a sign to those outside the church that they do not have to give way to despair. There is something stronger than evil they can trust. By becoming disciples of Jesus Christ, they can be formed in this hope too. The power of our hope should be so visible that it causes people to ask how we can be joyful when things look so dark. As 1 Peter 3:15 admonishes us, we should "always be ready to make [our] defense to anyone who demands from [us] an accounting for the hope that is in [us]."

One way we can demonstrate this hope is through praising God. As with the worship leader the First Church members heard, this praise should not be ignorant of the struggles people face. Rather, it should be an act of hopeful resistance. Instead of collapsing under the strain of the difficulties we face, we resist the power of despair by declaring our firm belief that God is good, and all things will be redeemed. We can do this on Sunday morning after terrible tragedies, during funerals, or in quiet prayers we share one-on-one with others. Congregations can even do it by teaching people songs that can sustain them in difficult times. Some of the old traditional songs like "His Eye Is on the Sparrow," "It Is Well with My Soul," and "Sweet Hour of Prayer" can be powerful in this way.

Praising God in hope can be more than just a sign to others that God will set things right. It can also be a means God uses to accomplish God's good purposes. Isaiah Freeman, former worship leader

137

at Willow Creek North Shore, uses the walls of Jericho to explain this. God commanded the warriors and priests of Israel to march around the city of Jericho with the priests blowing their horns. They did this for six days. On the seventh day, they marched around the city seven times. As they finished, Joshua told the people "Shout! For the LORD has given you the city. The people shouted, and the trumpets were blown. As soon as the people heard the sound of the trumpets, they raised a great shout, and the wall fell down flat; so the people charged straight ahead into the city and captured it" (Josh 6:16, 20).

Freeman said that shouting was an act of hope God used to overcome the obstacle facing the Israelites. It was in the very act of shouting their praise that God allowed them to claim what God had promised them.[3]

By being both hopeful and joyful we gain the capacity to praise God as we participate in God's mission, regardless of the situations around us. We can laugh with those who laugh, pointing to God as the Giver of all good things, and weep with those who weep, pointing to God as the Rock that holds firm and will one day restore all things. We can invite people to become disciples of Jesus Christ, who is big enough to handle everything we face.

Worship is the best activity for practicing hope and joy in our congregations. It provides us with multiple activities (prayer, music, the sermon, and other creative means) to acknowledge the struggles that are in front of us while still praising God. By doing this, worship becomes a missional act. It encourages Christians to remain hopeful and joyful as we go through our lives and interact with people. It also offers a powerful witness to those who may visit our worship, letting them know that Christians are not naive about the pains or pleasures of the world but see both these things in the light of God's goodness. One of the reasons we often do not invite friends to worship in our congregations is because we do not feel our congregations have anything meaningful to offer them. If our worship

---

3   Isaiah Freeman, homily at Willow Creek Community Church North Shore, Northbrook, IL, May 22, 2016.

is steeped in hope and joy, that will not be a problem. Our worship will be relevant and transformative.

Our administration should also be shaped by hope and joy. We may think administration is just about getting the business of the church done. However, by including a time of praise in these meetings, not just at the beginning and end but as something we do throughout the meeting to acknowledge the good things God has done and to offer to God our hopes for the future, we practice hope and joy. We lift before God the good things we have enjoyed and the struggles we face. We mature in our discipleship as we do this.

As God forms us to be more hopeful and joyful, we also become permission-giving through our administration. Committees are often focused on dealing with the status quo. Creating an administrative pipeline that not only welcomes people to bring their passions and excitement for ministry but that trains, equips, and provides resources to those people is an act of hope. It allows a congregation to expand its missional activity by supporting what God wants to do through those people.

The leaders of First Church experimented with all these ideas for several months. What they found was that living in a way that promoted the spiritual fruit of joy required learning new ways of living together. Until this point, they had always understood joy—along with the other fruits of the Spirit: love, peace, patience, kindness, goodness, faithfulness, gentleness, and self-control—as personal traits. Now they realized that while an individual might or might not demonstrate these fruits, it took an entire congregation to cultivate those fruits in each person's life.

By creating new ways of engaging with God and one another in their worship, their administration, and their fellowship time, they found themselves more equipped to be in mission. People who had never been in leadership before came forward because they were inspired to begin new ministries and knew that the leaders of First Church were ready to listen and support their ideas. For those who did not feel called to start formal ministries, the ability to relate to people outside the church during the pains and pleasures of life made them more effective evangelists. Because of this, several new people began coming to First Church.

The leaders of First Church had started by asking how could they get the people in the congregation to be more joyful. They thought the answer was going to be programmatic, leading them to new activities or changes in the congregation's structures. While both things happened, they had not anticipated that the question would take them to such a deep level of formation. However, that formation was exactly what they needed. It was God's way of sustaining them so they could continue to participate in the amazing missional work God had been doing through them. This was something truly worth celebrating!

Key Tactics: How to Celebrate

- Take time to give thanks to God for everything that goes well. You can do this during worship as well as in committee meetings. However you do it, remind people regularly of God's goodness to your congregation.

- Give everyone in the congregation a way to share about God's goodness to them. This could include during meals, through cards, on a website or blog, or any other way to acknowledge the good things God has done for those in the congregation.

- Think about physical pleasures and how you address them in your personal lives. Are you uncomfortable talking about them in church? Why? Consider how these are good gifts, and ways that embracing them as God's good gifts to you may change how you think and talk about them.

- Be hospitable to one another in your congregation, welcoming the opportunity to share about your whole lives, including what gives you pleasure.

- Acknowledge that people outside the church want to enjoy themselves, not judging them for it, and making room for them to talk about this unashamedly in your congregation.

- Show hospitality to people by sharing the best you have with them.

- Show hospitality to those who struggle with addiction by providing recovery groups. There are different recovery groups with different philosophies. Spend time researching which group fits best with your congregation's theology. Also, many courthouses have a person assigned to deal with people cited for alcohol infractions. Speaking to that person can help you get a sense for the recovery needs in your area.
- Praise God in your worship.
- Teach people to praise God on their own, such as by singing or reciting Scripture verses that speak to God's power and goodness.
- Equip people in the congregation to acknowledge the pain and tragedy those outside the church encounter, weep with them, and then lead them to recognize the hope of God overcoming these problems.
- Create administrative structures that include times to praise God for what God has done and pray for what you hope God will do to move the mission ahead.
- Create permission-giving structures that invite people to share their new ministry ideas with the congregation and get the necessary resources to support them.

THE SECRETS OF BEING A MISSIONAL CONGREGATION

1 Peter 3:21-22

Five years have rolled on since we were introduced to First Church. Much has happened in that time:

- Prayer has continued to be a consistent practice of the church. There are regular prayer meetings, members of the church are instructed on ways to pray and encouraged to pray individually, and each committee meeting involves prayer and praise throughout the agenda.
- Small groups have formed to encourage personal accountability in the congregation. These groups create spaces for members of the church to explain how they are seeking to live their Christian faith in daily life.
- Other groups have formed in the church to address specific issues in the town. These groups continue to work with the racism task force as well as with education, nutrition, and other issues. These groups also have proven to be helpful places for new people coming to the church to get involved and to build relationships with church members.
- The Hispanic female pastor is now well established and known in the town.

- First Pub Church is thriving. Many other congregations in the town have become interested in setting up similar sorts of gatherings. Rather than seeing this as competition, the members of FPC have worked with these other congregations. FPC emphasizes the importance of talking about the Christian faith and practicing their faith through service toward others.

- The town's racism task force has tackled several major historical injustices among the various neighborhoods in the town. While change is slow, the tenor of the conversation within the town has begun to shift. Notions of privilege and of systemic failures toward the Hispanic neighborhood have begun to be accepted concepts in town discussions. Some efforts are being made to generate private investment in the Hispanic neighborhood and to create more ways to connect that neighborhood physically with the rest of the town.

- The relationship between First Church and the Hispanic church has flourished. The members of both churches have begun to look forward to seeing each other at congregational events as well as informally. Some of the children are even requesting playdates and using both English and Spanish with each other, helping draw the adults closer to one another.

- The recovery ministries have grown substantially, and they have become an engine for growth in both congregations. The depth of substance abuse in the town had not been recognized before this; but with the hospitality the congregations have offered through these groups, many people are stepping forward and receiving the help they need.

- While the size of the town precludes a massive increase at First Church, the church still has attracted new people, invited them into the Christian faith, and begun the process of equipping them to be disciples of Jesus Christ.

- The existing members of First Church have become much more generous in their giving.
- A sense of joy and hope pervades the congregation. They realize that they have no guarantee of all going well in the coming years or even months. However, they trust that God will continue to supply all they need if they stay faithful in missional work.

In looking back over these changes, the members of First Church often chuckle to think that it all started in a moment of desperation. They needed to pay the bills and didn't have enough money. With nothing left to do, they had turned to God in prayer. That changed everything.

The pastor who had been at First Church at the beginning of this missional transformation picked up this theme in his remarks when he was invited back for the congregation's homecoming. He explained that never in their wildest dreams did he or the rest of the congregation think that they would find the power, wisdom, and faith to move into mission from what had been the lowest point in the congregation's history. At the time, they just wanted to survive. However, by channeling their uncertainty and fear into reliance on God rather than looking for a magic bullet that would fix them, they took the necessary steps to become missional. They found that being missional was less a matter of having the right answers and techniques than it was being prepared to follow God wherever God led. God was already in the world doing mission. The church just needed to serve alongside God, participating in the redemption of the world through the gifts God gave the church.

"Secrets" of Effective Mission
Disciples Make Disciples
First Church had learned in those early days, as well as in the days after the new pastor had come, that participation with God meant a change of heart. As the pastor put it, before Jesus commissioned his earliest followers to make disciples, he had spent years developing those followers as disciples. This was the great secret: *disciples make disciples,* and neither First Church nor any other congregation

could be effective in mission unless the people in that congregation began by submitting to become disciples of Jesus Christ.

Both Individuals and Congregations Make Disciples

God had used the desperation of First Church to bring the people to the point where they were willing to do this. Before then, the congregation was just comfortable enough, even in its steady decline, to avoid turning seriously to God. However, as exile from the building or even from existence as a congregation came close, the congregation relented and repented. The real danger because of the music director deepened this reliance on God, not allowing the congregation to go "back to normal" once the immediate financial pressures were alleviated. And after seeing the faithful love and power of God sustain them in their need, the leaders of First Church decided they didn't want to go "back to normal." They wanted to continue their new reliance on God both personally and corporately. This led them to another secret: *both individuals and congregations are needed to make disciples.*

The members of First Church had always thought of themselves as individual believers who gathered together because of common beliefs. The role of the congregation was to support them in these personal beliefs with instruction, inspiration, and some opportunities to practice their faith. In terms of mission, this meant that the congregation was supposed to equip the individual members to evangelize their neighbors. And, frankly, the congregation had not done such a great job of that.

However, as the congregation made its turn into being missional, and as the congregation members began to share their faith more, they found that one-on-one evangelism was not enough. The town needed a bigger public witness than what the individuals could present on their own. It needed the witness of a corporate body to address the corporate struggles of the town.

They first realized this when First Church got involved with the vacation Bible school in the Hispanic neighborhood. Addressing the issues of racism and injustice with individuals was important, but to make a dent in the economic and political inequality faced by the people in the Hispanic neighborhood required an entire congregation to stand in public witness for love of neighbor. As a congregation they could connect with other organizations and create a collective impact that was felt across the town in ways that individual volunteers could not. In addition, as a congregation they could give birth to new congregations. First Church had done this by first attracting the people in the pub with its public witness and then launching them as First Pub Church. This launch led to more launches, both in the formation of First Cantina Church and of other congregations the leaders of FPC helped.

Growing Mission = Growing Faith

As First Church had sought to be faithful with these opportunities, the pastor believed it had uncovered one other secret: *growing in mission goes hand-in-hand with growing in faith.* As the missional activities continued, the people in First Church began to feel God's Spirit calling them to reflect the character of God more fully. They wanted to experience God's joy, hope, and healing within their congregation and to share these virtues with others. This, the pastor concluded, was a never-ending process. Just as we can never exhaust knowing the eternal God, so we can never exhaust growing into God's likeness or participating in God's mission. Even with all it had done, First Church might have difficult days ahead of it. Being in mission did not mean God barred that from happening. It just meant that the congregation would deal with whatever came as those who were committed to being more faithful as disciples and to inviting others to become disciples.

More "Secrets" to Becoming Missional

In reflecting on First Church's experiences, the pastor uncovered the above three core secrets about becoming a missional congregation. We can add a few more.

Creativity

The activities First Church found itself using to be missional are not the ones that we usually think of when dealing with evangelism or mission. Yet, as we've seen, God sent the people of God on mission in different ways throughout the Bible. When Jesus pronounced the Great Commission, he did not wipe away those other ways of being in mission. He just made it clear that the primary work of the church is to make disciples, which includes baptizing and teaching. He never specified or limited how we should do those things.

Even the corporate activities of witnessing against racism and of being open to talking about physical pleasures are part of making disciples. While these activities do not directly invite people outside the church into discipleship, they

- provide a public witness people outside the church can observe;
- form the people in the church as disciples; and
- provide a means for redeeming the culture.

Each of these is necessary for making disciples.

Providing a public witness is essential if we want people to hear our message. Even if we are not directly inviting people to become disciples of Jesus Christ, we can present ourselves to those outside the church in a way that awakens them to the redemptive work of God. When they see us caring for those in need and creating a community in which all people are valued, they see us living the same way that Jesus did. This witness is the first step to building credibility with them. In time, that credibility will allow us to share the gospel with them and invite them to become disciples. This is living into the command Jesus gave in Acts 1:8, "You will be my witnesses."

The second point about deepening the discipleship of those already in the church is not as obvious but is no less important. Remember, the Great Commission tells us that we are to make disciples "as we are going." As we go through life, we encounter people who are Christians as well as those who are not. While Christians may already be disciples, we can still encourage them to grow in their discipleship. This is no less a way of fulfilling the Great Commission.

Some of the greatest evangelists in history focused on guiding Christians to grow as disciples. John Wesley, for example, preached to those who were already baptized members of the Church of England but who needed to become more intentional in seeking after scriptural holiness. Jonathan Edwards preached to those who were already Puritans but desired them to grow more deeply in their love of Jesus Christ. Even though their work was making disciples of those who were already in the church, these two preachers were clearly obedient to the Great Commission.

The last point about redeeming culture may seem strange. The Great Commission makes it sound as if our primary work is to make individuals into disciples of Jesus Christ. Yes, but making disciples is not God's final purpose. Ultimately, God seeks to redeem all creation by establishing the kingdom of God. The church is commissioned to make disciples so people can anticipate the day when God brings the kingdom in its fullness. Jesus himself made this point when he preached, "Repent, for the kingdom of heaven has come near" (Matt 4:17). He called us to make disciples so that those disciples could live in his coming kingdom.

Jesus not only commissions us to make disciples so we can participate in a future kingdom but to be disciples participating in that kingdom now. The way his earliest disciples organized themselves as a church after Pentecost demonstrates this. They built new kinds of communities that allowed for dignity to be given to men and women, such as the church in Antioch. These new communities began to redeem the culture and social structures by how they lived.

It is impossible for a congregation of disciples to avoid redeeming the larger culture and social structures if those disciples are obeying the Great Commission. Author Andy Crouch suggests that part of the mission we are called to is "culture making."[1] Theologian James Cone likewise argues that evangelism irreducibly requires engagement in politics.[2]

The early church demonstrated what this engagement looked like. As it made disciples, it formed a community that defined itself by love of God and love of neighbor. Over the centuries, the church

---

1   Andy Crouch. *Culture Making: Recovering Our Creative Calling* (Downers Grove, IL: IVP, 2008).

2   James H. Cone, "Evangelization and Politics: A Black Perspective," *Black Theology: A Documentary History,* vol. 2, 1980–1992, eds. James H. Cone and Gayraud S. Wilmore (Maryknoll, NY: Orbis, 1993), 531–42.

expanded its witness, prompting entire cultures and societies to examine how people are treated. One of the greatest global contributions of the church in doing this has been the establishment of human rights as we know them today.[3]

When looking at what creative ways of being in mission allow a congregation to do (provide a public witness people outside the church can observe, form the people in the church as disciples, and provide means for redeeming the culture), it becomes clear that obedience to the Great Commission can and should reach beyond the stereotypical ideas we often associate with missions. This does not dilute or minimize Christ's commission for the church to make disciples but expands how that commission ripples out to encompass a wide array of activities.

Sacrifice

Throughout its journey to being missional, First Church needed to make some difficult decisions, such as joining the joint vacation Bible school in the park or letting go of the members who could not follow the congregation in mission. This reminds us that, while God does amazing things through those who commit themselves to making disciples, being faithful to that mission often entails sacrifice.

Sacrifice is interwoven with mission. Even Jesus had to sacrifice to complete the work God sent him to do. Paul reminds us, in Philippians 2:6-8, Jesus, "who, though he was in the form of God, did not regard equality with God as something to be exploited, but emptied himself, taking the form of a slave, being born in human likeness. And being found in human form, he humbled himself and became obedient to the point of death—even death on a cross." Only after this sacrifice "God also highly exalted him and gave him the name that is above every name" (v. 9).

If Jesus had to sacrifice to participate in the mission of God, how much more shall we!

---

3   Mike Aquilina and James L. Papandrea, *Seven Revolutions: How Christianity Changed the World and Can Change It Again* (New York: Image, 2015), 6.

But what sort of sacrifice does God ask our congregations to make to be missional? While the Scripture is clear that the mission of God can demand that we sacrifice our wealth, our freedom, or even our lives, what we most often sacrifice is our comfort. Many of our congregations have become comfortable being ineffective at making disciples. Even with all the tactics available to be missional, we settle into a pattern that serves our interests rather than Christ's commission.

If we are serious about being missional congregations, we sacrifice that comfort. This can be disorienting. It might feel as if we are moving from our native culture to a foreign culture, having to learn new traditions that are strange and unusual to us. We might need to become accustomed to new forms of music, new kinds of food, new timetables, new ways of organizing, new venues for engaging in ministry, new people we have not had in our congregations before, and a new sense of what responsibilities we have as Christians.

For some of our congregations, the buildings themselves are hindrances to mission. We spend nearly everything to keep the facilities from crashing down on us, and we know they are not attractive for new people to enter. It may be that we are called to sacrifice our buildings so we can free the finances and energy we are putting into maintaining them to focus on making disciples. How many city hall meetings could we attend if we had fewer trustee meetings dealing with deferred maintenance? How many more houses for the homeless could we construct if we spent fewer hours patching the old HVAC system? How much money could go to evangelism if we didn't have to keep the extra amount on hand because the roof might spring another leak?

Many congregations resist these sacrifices, thinking they will lose what it means to be a church by losing those comfortable ways of operating. In fact, our sacrifices help us focus on what is most valuable to a congregation: relationships and faith. Making disciples calls us deeper into each of these. It brings us closer to God as we rely more heavily on God to transform ourselves and others, and it draws us deeper into relationships with God and with those inside and outside of the church. We encourage one another in our faith inside the church and share the good news of Jesus with those outside the church.

Even though we are reclaiming what is most important to us as a congregation when we become more missional, letting go of buildings, traditions, and rituals can hurt. It is a sacrifice, but one that is worth it. As Jesus said, "When a woman is in labor, she has pain, because her hour has come. But when her child is born, she no longer remembers the anguish because of the joy of having brought a human being into the world. So you have pain now; but I will see you again, and your hearts will rejoice, and no one will take your joy from you" (John 16:21-22).

The things we hold on to in our congregations often do not bring us joy. Going through the pain of letting go of whatever stands in the way of mission will free us to be filled with joy. We will not be weighed down by the cares of the past and present, but will be hopeful for what God can do with us in the future as we draw closer to each other and to God.

Leadership and Gifts

Leaders were essential characters throughout the story of First Church. This included the pastors but also the various lay leaders who came alongside the two pastors. They took the initial steps to be formed as disciples through spiritual disciplines and from that saw the opportunities for the congregation to increase its public witness. They also made the hard decisions and accepted the risk their decisions entailed.

The most important quality for leaders in a missional congregation, both lay and clergy, is faithfulness. How the leaders practice their faith in their daily lives and how they conduct the activities of the church will set a pattern for the congregation.[4] Leaders should be selected first on whether they will be exemplars for what the congregation wants to become.

This is not to suggest that congregations should be led in a top-down

---

4   Rick Richardson, who teaches evangelism at Wheaton College, has found that congregations cannot become missionally vibrant unless their leaders experience accountability, inspiration, and instruction in personal witness every thirty days. He recommends that church leaders, especially senior pastors, join a cohort of other leaders who will provide this. This will set the example for how the rest of the congregation practices their faith. Rick Richardson, "Local Church Culture & Evangelistic Witness, Engaging Senior Leaders (part 2 of 4)," *Re-Kindle: Engaging in Gospel Conversations,* November 18, 2015, https://www.youtube.com /watch?v=HDcXzxRneqs.

model. Different missional congregations should choose governing structures that fit best with how they operate. Whatever structure is chosen, though, missional congregations should always be diligent to discern those who have leadership gifts in their midst and to give them opportunities to grow in those gifts. This becomes the basis for multiplying congregations, as each congregation recognizes new leaders and nurtures them so they can be sent out and establish new congregations.

Alan Hirsch suggests in his book *The Permanent Revolution* that the primary gifts God has given Christians for the mission of the church are laid out in Ephesians 4:11-13: "The gifts he gave were that some would be apostles, some prophets, some evangelists, some pastors and teachers, to equip the saints for the work of ministry, for building up the body of Christ, until all of us come to the unity of the faith and of the knowledge of the Son of God, to maturity, to the measure of the full stature of Christ."[5] According to Hirsch, apostles see visions of where God wants the gospel to go and proclaim the gospel in those places. Prophets recognize the differences between the truth of God and cultural values, providing a corrective voice for how God would have people live. Evangelists welcome people into the Christian faith. Pastors, or what Hirsch refers to as "shepherds," nurture people in the faith. Teachers understand and explain the faith to those who are already within the church.[6]

Hirsch argues that all these gifts are necessary for a congregation to be missional. While the governing leaders do not need to have any one of these gifts, each person in a congregation should know what his or her gifts are, so he or she can step forward and provide leadership in missional activities when necessary.

Hirsch believes all these gifts build on one another to sustain the missional work of the church. Without apostles leading the charge to share the gospel in new places, congregations cannot be established. Without prophets clarifying God's truth in relation to the culture, congregations can lose their faithfulness to the gospel,

---

5   Alan Hirsch and Tim Catchim, *The Permanent Revolution: Apostolic Imagination and Practice for the 21st Century Church* (San Francisco: Jossey-Bass, 2012), 7–8.

6   Ibid., 9.

and evangelists will not have a worthwhile community to invite people to join. Without evangelists, no one becomes a Christian or joins a congregation, so there is no need to nurture or teach. Without shepherding, people do not feel loved and do not stay for the teaching. Without teaching, no one who stays in the church matures in faith.[7]

According to Hirsch, mainline denominational congregations have de-emphasized the gifts of apostles, prophets, and evangelists.[8] Historically, they valued all five gifts, but over time the emphasis on being a comfortable institutional structure drove out or silenced the people with the first three. Without the apostolic gift of moving beyond the walls of the church with the gospel, the prophetic voice to differentiate between God's will and cultural values, and the evangelistic gift of inviting people to become followers of Jesus Christ, these congregations became nothing but groups of people who love and teach one another. That may sound nice, but it is not missional.[9] It is akin to the fictional story at the beginning of the book in which Jesus never delivered the Great Commission.

Compounding the problem, the shepherding and teaching roles tend to be reserved for those with specific expertise. This means that most people in the church are treated as no more than consumers of pastoral care and pastoral teaching. The result is to kill any missional capacity that a congregation might have. To be a missional congregation requires everyone to get involved in making disciples. There is no room for people to be consumers only, except for those who are so new to the Christian faith that they need to learn the basic contours of their commitment to Jesus Christ. Even that teaching, though, should be imbued with the call for these new Christians to get active in God's mission.

The only reason that the mainline denominations have survived so long without the outward-looking gifts is that they grew

---

7   Ibid., 115.

8   Ibid., 17–20.

9   Alan Hirsch, "The Overlooked Leadership Roles," *Leadership Journal* Spring 2008, http://www.christianitytoday.com/le/2008/spring/7.32.html?start=1.

large and wealthy thanks to the earlier missional movements that birthed them. They also fed off a supportive culture. However, now that the culture has changed, those of us who pastor existing mainline congregations are reaping the result of being focused on inward activities: trying to keep the institution going while fighting back the nagging fear we will one day disappear from lack of new people joining us. And the denominations will disappear without new congregations being planted in new locations to replace the ones that are closing.

Leadership drawing from all five gifts is essential to bring us back from this dangerous edge. We need it to lead our congregations into mission as well as to lead our denominations back to health as participants in the Great Commission.

Brings Us Back to the Great Commission

In pronouncing the Great Commission, Jesus launched the church to participate in God's work of redeeming creation by making disciples. The church was to invite these new disciples into a community of Christians through baptism and teach them what Jesus had taught, demonstrating to the world what the kingdom of God looks like. Jesus left the door wide open for how the church could carry out this work.

Being missional does not start with techniques for persuading people to become Christians or impressing people with great programs or even with planting new churches, but with God's power transforming our character. As we have seen in tracking the experiences of First Church, every move toward tactics requires a deeper dive into our own discipleship. A hypocrite or lukewarm Christian might be able to work for justice or preach a good sermon, but demonstrating a consistent public witness that will attract people to become disciples of Jesus Christ requires one to have a committed faith.

Congregations are an indispensable unit of witness God uses to form disciples. They are the local community of faith that provides a witness to God's goodness by how it engages the culture and social structures around it, welcomes individuals to become disciples, demonstrates how people can pattern their lives by loving God and loving neighbor, and launches those new disciples into the world as agents of reconciliation. By living this way, congregations become the sign of God's kingdom for those outside the church to see, a foretaste of what the kingdom is like for those who join it, and an instrument God uses to advance that kingdom in the world.

Becoming a Great Commission congregation begins when we yield everything about our congregation to the Holy Spirit. Only then do we determine what missional tactics best suit our congregation's gifts and context. This may require rethinking the kinds of activities our congregations get involved in, redefining how we carry out the ministries we already do, or sacrificing things that have made our congregations comfortable for a long time. Practically speaking, it may also require looking to our denominational leaders for help or helping those leaders understand the new vision that our congregation has for becoming missional if they are uncomfortable with the changes we want to make.

All of this is an admittedly difficult move for existing congregations. In some cases, it is like recasting ourselves as a new church start, integrating the Great Commission into everything we do. That is the only way to do it, however. Much as we would like to, we cannot cram missional activities into what we are already doing or assign those activities to a committee while the rest of the congregation's life continues unaffected. As Jesus explained, we need new wineskins for new wine. For many of us, understanding the Great Commission this way is new wine compared to the comfortable decline we have experienced. Our congregational structures, policies, and procedures need to change if we are to live into it—and so do our denominations, creating the space for these kinds of congregational realignments with the Great Commission.

The missional tactics in this book, then, are not a list of best practices meant to generate church growth. Rather, they are meant to provide practical steps for congregations that have already decided to commit to discipleship internally so they can be more effective at making disciples of Jesus Christ in the world. And they are a call to that commitment for those congregations that have not yet made it.

As uncomfortable as taking the step to become Great Commission congregations may be, we do not engage in God's mission alone. We follow a path that Jesus walked first as the sent God. This is a path with a sure outcome if we remain faithful to God's purposes. First Peter 3:21-22 assures us of the final success Jesus enjoyed, describing him as "Jesus Christ, who has gone into heaven and is at the right hand of God, with angels, authorities, and powers made subject to him." For all the pain, sacrifice, and difficulty we may have to face, we are promised that the path of mission is a path that leads to glory. And, if we do it right, we will know great hope and joy along the way.

AFTERWORD AND ADDITIONAL RESOURCES

This book provides solid guidance for how an existing congregation can become missional. However, it is admittedly a bit arbitrary, offering creative tactics to become missional based on the fictional story of First Church. This was intentional, in hopes that your congregation would find resonance with some part of First Church's story, giving you an entry point to think about how your congregation could become more missional.

To provide as many entry points as possible, I touch on many items in the book, such as working for racial justice, leadership development, and planting new churches, without getting into the details of how to execute them. One I want to revisit briefly here is multiplication, a concept the pastor brings up very briefly during the sermon in the final chapter.

We often think about missional congregations welcoming new people. This sort of welcoming is growth by addition: a local congregation that attracts new people and adds them to its membership. In the book, I point to addition, but I also gesture in the direction of multiplication. Multiplication occurs when a congregation launches new congregations. The original congregation equips and sends out apostolic leaders who plant new congregations that, in turn, will equip and send out apostolic leaders to plant newer congregations.

This is multiplication: creating a movement of congregations that plant new congregations.

The logic of multiplication is that each congregation should understand itself as pregnant. It is pregnant with the ability to birth a new congregation from the moment it is planted. It just needs to provide the new life within its sufficient resources and then go through the process of letting that new life enter the world to become a freestanding congregation of its own. Much of the missional guidance in this book encourages this sort of ecclesiastical pregnancy, especially the emphasis on discipleship. So if your congregation tracks with the ideas in the book you will be in good shape to start multiplying![1]

There are more focused resources that can go deeper on the tactics I have raised in this book and that can walk you through how to use them. Below is a list of online resources, including organizations, conferences, blogs, podcasts, and periodicals that offer consistent and high-quality information for people who want to be part of a missional church. Since the missional movement is so vibrant, tracking with these sites, in addition to reading books, will help keep you abreast of the most important developments and thinking about all things missional.

Academy for Evangelism in Theological Education (AETE). AETE is the primary academic guild dealing with evangelism. It welcomes students, professors, and practitioners to annual meetings and includes both evangelicals and mainline Protestants. It also publishes a peer-reviewed online journal entitled *Witness*. The archive of *Witness* is free to access.

- Main site: https://aete.online/
- *Witness* site: http://journals.sfu.ca/witness/index.php/witness/index

---

1   For those who trace their theological lineage back to John Wesley, you will recognize the multiplication idea. The entire structure of the Methodist Revival promoted the multiplication of faith communities. James Logan offers an excellent overview of this in his brief book *How Great a Flame* (Nashville: Discipleship Resources, 2014).

American Society of Missiology (ASM). While not just focused on evangelism, ASM provides a larger academic context for discussing evangelism among missionaries, missiology scholars, and students. They also publish texts and the journal *Missiology*.

- http://asmweb.org/

Amplify. Amplify is a conference hosted annually by the Billy Graham Center for Evangelism. It welcomes some of the top practitioners in the missional church movement, provides the latest new research on evangelism, and publishes videos of its plenary sessions for free access.

- http://www.amplifyconference.tv/

The Association of Religion Data Archives (the ARDA). An enormous database of virtually every major study done concerning religion from a wide variety of reputable sources (for example, Pew Research Center), many dealing with how people feel about the church and the Christian faith.

- http://thearda.com/

Billy Graham Center for Evangelism (BGCE). The BGCE is a leading voice in scholarship and new research around evangelism. They regularly host conferences that bring evangelism scholars and practitioners together. They also have made a substantial amount of evangelism expertise and insight available free online, including through the Gospel Life blog and the Rekindle: Engaging Gospel Conversations Youtube channel that they jointly host with Q Place.

- http://www.wheaton.edu/BGCE

Christianity Today and Outreach Magazine. *Christianity Today* focuses on cultural analysis and how Christians can maintain a faithful public witness. *Outreach Magazine* deals with church planting and evangelism practices for especially smaller congregations.

- http://www.christianitytoday.com/
- http://www.outreachmagazine.com/

Discipleship Ministries of The United Methodist Church. Discipleship Ministries oversees all discipleship-making activities in The

United Methodist Church. They have a dedicated staff member who directs evangelism activities and who also provides several resources about evangelism. In 2015, they cosponsored a series of webinars with the World Council of Churches on evangelism available online.

- http://www.umcdiscipleship.org/resources /world-council-of-churches-evangelism-webinars

They also are the organization that oversees Path1, which is the United Methodist program that launches and equips new church starts.

- http://www.umcdiscipleship.org/new-church-starts

Exponential. Exponential aggregates and distributes content from ministries that are focused on specific areas of church multiplication via content "channels." These channels focus on items such as developing multiethnic congregations (mosaix), negotiating culture, and planting multisite churches.

- https://exponential.org/

Foundation for Evangelism. The Foundation was developed as a group of laypeople who felt strongly about the need for evangelism to be included in theological education. They have endowed several professorships in evangelism, supported campus ministries, provided fellowships for doctoral students focusing on evangelism, and encouraged local United Methodist congregations to be more evangelistic with their annual evangelism awards.

- http://foundationforevangelism.org/

Lifeway Research. A major Christian research group focused on gathering statistics about Christians, the church, and the relationship between those outside the church and the Christian faith.

- http://lifewayresearch.com/

Mosaix. A group dedicated to the development of multiethnic faith communities that offers resources, an annual gathering, and personal coaching.

- http://www.mosaix.info/

NewChurches.com. Run by Daniel Im of LifeWay Research and Ed Stetzer of the Billy Graham Center for Evangelism, NewChurches .com provides weekly blogs and podcasts that deal with a wide variety of issues facing missional congregations. From planting a new church, to fund-raising, to making discipleship a priority, you can find almost every aspect of missional life on this website. It includes both free and subscription level access, along with the ability to search podcasts and blogs for specific topics.

- https://newchurches.com/

Verge Network. This network, developed in part by Alan Hirsch, focuses on leadership, discipleship, and practical steps for developing "incarnational missional communities of faith." With free registration, you can gain access to a library of pdfs written by the leaders of several high-profile missional congregations detailing their approach to ministry.

- http://www.vergenetwork.org/

World Council of Churches. The WCC publishes regular materials on evangelism, including major documents that bring together the best thinking of a wide variety of Christian voices about evangelism. This is a link to the 2012 document "Together Towards Life: Mission and Evangelism in Changing Landscapes."

- http://www.oikoumene.org/en/resources/ documents/commissions/mission-and-evangelism/ together-towards-life-mission-and-evangelism-in- changing-landscapes/

INDEX

Aaron, 21–22, 25–27, 36, 40–42, 111, 124
addiction, 130; recovery ministries, 134–35, 141
administration, 139, 141
advocacy, 27–29, 33, 74, 82–83, 92, 108–9
alcohol, 30–31, 111, 129, 132, 134–35, 141
Antioch, Church at, 94–95, 103, 112
apostle, gift of, 153–55

Babylon, 72, 76, 83–85, 120
best practices, 156
buildings (church facilities), 87–90, 92, 151–52; and worship, 40, 44

celebration, xvii, 3, 34, 37, 83, 87, 108, 112, 117–18, 120–28, 130–32, 135–36, 140

character, xxi, 35, 110, 126–27, 147, 155
Chesterton, G. K., 118–19
collective impact, 29, 147
committees, xii, xv, xvii, xxviii–xxix, 3, 20–21, 42, 49, 55, 124, 126, 139–40, 143, 156
consecration, 36–39, 41–43, 46, 49, 111
context, for ministry, xxiii, xxvi, 47, 69, 104, 156; and Scripture, 87; in North America, xix, xxii
culture, xx, xxvii, 78, 81–82, 86, 102, 121, 148–51, 154–55

David, 2, 12–13, 47, 117
discernment, xvii, xx, xxv, 15, 22, 49, 57, 62–63, 69, 76, 153
disciple making, xi–xii, xiv, xv–xvi, xix–xx, xxii, xxv–xxvii, xxx, 1, 4, 27, 34, 41, 48, 73,

79, 81, 92, 95, 104, 121, 129–
     30, 145–46, 148–50
diversity, 94–95, 106–8, 110–
     13, 114
Donne, John, xxix–xxx

Ecclesiastes, 117, 127–29
Edwards, Jonathan, 149
evangelism, xi, xxiii, 17–18, 39,
     44–47, 50, 146–47, 149, 151
evangelist, gift of, 153–55
evil, x, 2–3, 18, 35, 52, 62, 120,
     129, 136–37
exile, xvii, 47, 71–92, 146
existing congregations, 106, 156

facilities, 87–89
false teaching, 83–87
finances, xxv, 3, 20, 81, 151
food, 21, 23–25, 41, 81, 103–4,
     108, 130–34, 151
Footloose, 117
front page test, 61, 69

gifts, spiritual, xxii, xxx, 54, 61–62,
     69, 79, 145, 152–56; physical
     pleasers as, 130–31, 134,
     136, 140
Great Commission, v–vii, x–xii,
     xiv, xx–xxi, xxv, xxx, 1, 19, 37,
     68, 79–80, 89, 95, 111–12,
     129–30, 148–50, 154–57

healing, ix, xxiv, xxv, 2, 99–100
hiding, xvii, 3, 10, 12–15, 53, 87
Hirsch, Alan, 153–54

holiness, xx, 36, 41–42, 73, 124,
     149
hope, x, xv, 14, 25, 120, 135–39,
     141, 145, 147, 157
hospitality, 133–34, 141, 144
hostility, 69

idolatry, 76–79
injustice, xvi, xxii, 82–83, 90,
     105, 109, 113, 135, 144, 146

Joshua, 31–32, 35, 45–46, 138
joy, ix–x, 118, 125–27, 145, 147,
     152, 157; and enjoyment, 119–
     20; and hope, 135–40; and
     mission, 120–22; as a witness,
     132–35
joy-killers, 128–29
justice, xii, 34, 80–83, 92, 93,
     103–4, 155, 159

kingdom of God, x, xiii–xv, xvi,
     xix, 29, 35, 53, 79, 113, 124,
     149, 155–56

leaders, xxiii, 8–9, 20, 22, 24,
     30, 64, 66–67, 74–76, 90–
     91, 122–24, 135, 139–40,
     146–47; and failure, 125;
     and gifts, 152–56; and idol-
     atry, 77; and reconciliation,
     96–99; and worship, 39–43,
     49–50; in the Church at An-
     tioch, 94
leisure, 80, 125
listening to other people, 58–60,

98, 102–4, 113–14, 131

local congregations, xi–xii, xvi, xxii–xxiii, xxvii

martyrs, 13, 51–52, 61

McNeil, Brenda Salter, 93, 103, 110, 112, 115

Moses, xiii, 19, 21–22, 25–28, 40, 45, 86, 124–25, 127

multiplication of churches, 153, 159–60

music, xvii, 38, 40, 42, 46, 133, 138, 151

news conference, 66–68

opposition, 1, 2, 53, 57, 60–61, 69–70, 96

Ott, Craig, xiii

parables: the lost sheep, the lost coin, and the Prodigal Son, 120–22

pastor, xi, xxviii, 42, 49–50, 59, 64, 69–70, 152–55

Path1, 89

patience, 13–14, 64, 109, 126, 139

Paul, xix–xx, xxv, 2, 61–62, 73, 77–78, 94, 120, 150,

perseverance, 13–14, 19, 34, 53, 57, 60–64, 68, 70

physical pleasure, 129–34, 137, 140, 148

Pilate, 53

politics, xxvi, 24–25, 27–29, 30,

33, 56–57, 74, 77, 83, 93–94, 98, 102, 114, 147, 149

Polycarp, 51–52

praise, 13–14, 16, 36, 42–43, 46, 132, 136–39, 141

prayer, 2–3, 14–15, 32, 69, 99, 137–38, 143; and advocacy, 29, 83; and fasting, 16; and spiritual warfare, 62, 64; and worship, 39, 42, 126; in committees, 20–22, 55–56

pregnant church, xx, 160

privilege, xxv, 27, 102–5, 113–14, 144

programs, xii, xv, xvii, xxiv, xxviii–xix, 20, 126, 140, 155

prophet, gift of, 153–55

protection by God, 2, 10–15, 16, 63, 69, 88

provision by God, 2, 4–10, 16, 55, 89

public meetings, 27, 58, 69

racism, 67–68, 73, 96, 106–7, 109, 123, 135, 143–44, 146, 148

Rahab, 31–32

reconciliation: with God, 96–99; with other people, 99–105

refugees, 71, 90

relationship: and reconciliation, 93, 95, 98, 100–102, 105, 110–12, 114; with God, xii, 98–99, 101, 151; with people in power, 26–27, 34; with un-churched people, xxii, 33, 79;

within the church, 46
resistance to church, 34, 60–61
retreat, 1–15, 49, 52–53, 132
Richardson, Rick, xi, 152n

Sabbath, xiii–xiv, 6–8
sacrifice, xv, 63, 73, 100, 118, 130, 150–52, 157
Samaritan, 18–19
scandal, 17, 19, 30, 33, 122
seeker-friendly/sensitive, 34, 40, 43
self-centeredness, 79–83
Sending God, xiii, 22
Sent God, xiii, xv, 22, 99, 157
sex, v, 111, 129–33
shepherd, gift of, 153–55
sin, xiv–xv, 18, 29–30, 41, 57, 64, 73, 79, 84, 90–91, 97–99, 120, 125–26, 129–34
Slaughter, Mike, 89–90
social structures, xxvi, 78, 102, 149, 156; and agendas, 77, 98; and categories, 78, 93, 102; and consciousness, 54; and justice, 82, 92; and media, 48, 67, 70
solidarity, 22–29, 34, 81, 83, 90

Stetzer, Ed, xi, xvii, 85–86
suffering, x, 26, 53, 63–64, 69, 80

teacher, gift of, 153–55

unchurched, 18, 82

vice, 18, 111
weakness, 7, 10, 12

Wesley, John, vi, xx, 63, 87, 148–49, 160n
Wesleyan Quadrilateral, 87
witness, xvi, xxiii, xxiv, 1, 4–8, 10, 14–16, 37–38, 41, 43, 46–47, 52–53, 57, 61, 63, 65, 67–68, 69–70, 72, 75, 83, 85–86, 90, 95, 110, 113, 123, 127, 138, 146–48, 150, 152, 155
worship, xvii, xxii, 35–39, 49–50, 111, 122, 131, 138–39, 140–41; and evangelism, 44–48; and leaders, 39–44

Yoder, John Howard, 11–12

CPSIA information can be obtained
at www.ICGtesting.com
Printed in the USA
LVOW03s1710210717
542002LV00001B/8/P